MW00897252

2025

# BLACKSTONE GRIDDLE

## COOKBOOK

2000 Days of Easy, Tasty and Gourmet Recipes Book For Beginners and Experts |
Step-by-Step Instructions for Unforgettable BBQ and Outdoor Grilling

*Stujikaislava Slavierilaow*

**Copyright© 2024 By Stujikaislava Slavierilaow**

**All rights reserved worldwide.**

No part of this book may be reproduced or transmitted in any form or by any means, electronic or mechanical, including photo- copying, recording or by any information storage and retrieval system, without written permission from the publisher, except for the inclusion of brief quotations in a review.

**Warning-Disclaimer**

The purpose of this book is to educate and entertain. The author or publisher does not guarantee that anyone following the techniques, suggestions, tips, ideas, or strategies will become successful. The author and publisher shall have neither liability or responsibility to anyone with respect to any loss or damage caused, or alleged to be caused, directly or indirectly by the information contained in this book.

# TABLE OF CONTENTS

# INTRODUCTION

In recent years, the Blackstone griddle has taken outdoor cooking by storm, captivating the hearts and taste buds of home cooks, professional chefs, and grilling enthusiasts alike. With its flat, expansive cooking surface and versatile heat distribution, the Blackstone griddle allows you to cook everything from traditional barbecue fare to delicate vegetables, breakfast spreads, and even desserts. This cookbook is dedicated to unlocking the full potential of your Blackstone griddle, providing you with a wide range of recipes and techniques that will elevate your outdoor cooking experience.

## The Appeal of Griddle Cooking

Griddle cooking has a rich history that spans across various cultures, where flat, heated surfaces have been used for centuries to cook food evenly and quickly. From the sizzling teppanyaki grills in Japan to the iconic American diner griddles, the Blackstone griddle represents a modern take on these timeless cooking methods. What sets the Blackstone apart is its ability to offer a perfect balance between heat control, cooking space, and ease of use.

One of the standout features of a Blackstone griddle is its ability to handle multiple dishes simultaneously. With a large, flat surface, you can grill burgers on one side, sauté vegetables on the other, and even toast buns all at once. This multitasking capability makes it ideal for large family gatherings, cookouts, and even weeknight dinners where speed and convenience are essential. Plus, the griddle's surface ensures consistent, even heating across its entirety, so every bite of food is perfectly cooked.

# Why the Blackstone Griddle is Different

Unlike traditional grills, which rely on an open flame and grates, the Blackstone griddle provides a smooth, flat surface that eliminates flare-ups and the risk of food falling through the gaps. It also allows for more cooking techniques, such as frying, searing, sautéing, and steaming, which may be more difficult to achieve on a standard grill. This versatility opens up a whole new world of culinary possibilities. Whether you're craving a perfectly seared steak, crispy bacon, or caramelized onions, the Blackstone griddle delivers consistent results every time.

The griddle's ability to retain heat also makes it a great tool for achieving those sought-after crispy textures and deep flavors. Foods like pancakes, hash browns, and smash burgers develop a delectable crust that is hard to replicate with other cooking methods. Plus, the griddle is highly responsive to temperature changes, allowing you to shift between high-heat searing and gentle simmering effortlessly.

# Cooking Beyond the Backyard BBQ

When most people think of outdoor cooking, their minds often drift toward the traditional backyard barbecue staples like burgers, hot dogs, and steaks. While the Blackstone griddle is certainly a champion at grilling up these favorites, its capabilities go far beyond the basics. This cookbook will show you how to make everything from gourmet breakfast feasts to globally inspired dishes, proving that the Blackstone griddle is not just for weekend barbecues but for every meal of the day.

Picture a lazy Sunday morning where the aroma of sizzling bacon and freshly flipped pancakes wafts through the air. Or imagine preparing a full taco spread with sizzling carne asada, grilled vegetables, and toasted tortillas all cooked on the same surface. The griddle's generous size makes it possible to cook for a crowd without sacrificing quality, ensuring that everyone gets to enjoy their meal hot and fresh off the grill.

Whether you're preparing breakfast, lunch, dinner, or dessert, the Blackstone griddle opens the door to endless culinary creativity. In this cookbook, you'll find recipes that transform everyday ingredients into extraordinary meals. From perfectly seared salmon to fluffy scrambled eggs, this griddle can handle it all with ease.

# Griddle Maintenance: An Essential Step

While the Blackstone griddle offers many advantages, proper care and maintenance are key to maximizing its longevity and performance. Just as a cast-iron skillet improves with use and care, so too does the Blackstone griddle. This cookbook will guide you through the essential steps of seasoning your griddle, cleaning it after each use, and protecting it from the elements to ensure that it remains a reliable tool for years to come.

A well-seasoned griddle not only enhances the nonstick properties of the surface but also infuses your food with that unmistakable griddle flavor that keeps people coming back for more. Regular maintenance is a small investment of time that pays off in perfectly cooked meals and a longer-lasting griddle.

## The Joy of Outdoor Cooking

At its core, cooking on the Blackstone griddle is about more than just preparing meals; it's about creating an experience. Outdoor cooking has a unique ability to bring people together, whether it's for a casual family dinner, a neighborhood cookout, or a celebratory feast. The sizzle of food hitting the griddle, the laughter of friends and family, and the anticipation of a delicious meal all combine to make outdoor cooking a truly special occasion.

With the Blackstone griddle, you're not limited by the season or the occasion. Whether it's a summer barbecue, a fall brunch, or even a quick weeknight dinner, the griddle is versatile enough to handle any situation. And with the wide variety of recipes included in this cookbook, you'll have the tools and inspiration to make the most of every meal.

## What to Expect in This Cookbook

This *Blackstone Griddle Cookbook* is designed to help you get the most out of your griddle, no matter your skill level. Whether you're a seasoned pro or new to griddle cooking, the recipes and tips included here will guide you through everything from the basics to more advanced techniques. You'll find sections dedicated to breakfast, lunch, and dinner, with a focus on easy-to-follow recipes that make the most of the griddle's capabilities.

We'll also explore some unexpected uses for your Blackstone griddle, such as preparing sweet treats like caramelized fruit or even baking flatbreads and pizzas. The recipes are designed to inspire creativity, so don't be afraid to experiment with different flavors and techniques. The goal is to make outdoor cooking not only accessible but also fun and rewarding.

# Chapter

# 1

# Breakfasts

# Chapter 1 Breakfasts

## Classic French Toast

**Prep time: 5 minutes | Cook time: 10 minutes | Serves 4**

- 6 eggs, beaten
- ¼ cup "half and half" or heavy cream
- 8 slices thick cut white or sourdough bread
- 2 tablespoons sugar
- 1 tablespoon cinnamon
- 1 teaspoon salt - butter
- powdered sugar
- maple syrup

1. Preheat your griddle to medium heat. 2. In a large mixing bowl, whisk together the eggs, cream, sugar, cinnamon, and salt until the mixture is smooth and well-blended. 3. Lightly coat the griddle with butter or vegetable oil. 4. Dip each slice of bread into the egg mixture, ensuring it's fully soaked, and place it on the griddle. 5. Once the French toast turns golden brown on one side, flip and cook the other side until it's browned, which should take around four minutes. Remove from the griddle, dust with powdered sugar, and serve with warm maple syrup.

## Grilled Ham & Swiss Crepes

**Prep time: 8 minutes | Cook time:12 minutes | Serves 2**

- 2 tablespoons oil
- ½ red bell pepper, thinly sliced
- 6 thin slices Black Forest
- ham
- 4 thin slices Swiss cheese
- 2 prepared crepes
- 2 teaspoons Dijon mustard

1. Preheat the griddle to medium and heat the oil. Sauté the bell pepper strips for 5 to 7 minutes, until they soften and wilt. Set aside and keep them warm. 2. Lay the ham slices flat on the griddle and heat them for around 5 minutes on one side. Flip the ham, then stack them into two piles of three overlapping slices. 3. Place two slices of cheese on top of each ham pile, add a few tablespoons of water to the griddle, and cover briefly to allow the cheese to melt. 4. While the cheese is melting, warm the crepes on the griddle and evenly spread half the mustard on each crepe. Top with the ham, melted cheese, and sautéed bell peppers. Fold the crepes and serve immediately.

## Toad in a Hole

**Prep time: 10 minutes | Cook time: 5 minutes | Serves 4**

- 4 slices white, wheat, or sourdough bread
- 4 eggs
- 2 tablespoons butter
- salt and black pepper

1. Preheat the griddle to medium heat and add the butter, spreading it evenly across the surface. 2. Cut a circular hole in the center of each bread slice. 3. Place the bread slices on the griddle and carefully crack an egg into the hole of each slice. 4. Cook until the bread is golden brown on the bottom, then flip and continue cooking until the egg whites are set. 5. Remove from the griddle, season with salt and black pepper, and serve immediately.

## Golden Corn Pancakes

**Prep time: 10 minutes | Cook time: 6 minutes | Serves 1**

- 2 eggs
- 1⅓ cups milk
- 1 tablespoon honey
- ¼ cup cooking oil
- 1½ cups all-purpose flour
- ½ cup fine cornmeal
- 4 teaspoons baking powder
- 1 tablespoon sugar
- 1 teaspoon salt

1. In a medium bowl, vigorously whisk together the eggs, milk, honey, and oil until they become light and frothy. In a separate large bowl, mix the flour, cornmeal, baking powder, sugar, and salt until thoroughly combined. 2. Gradually fold the wet mixture into the dry ingredients, stirring until smooth and free of lumps. Let the batter rest for 20 minutes while the grill preheats. 3. Set the griddle to medium-high heat. Lightly grease the surface with oil, heating it until the oil shimmers but doesn't smoke. 4. Pour about ¼ cup of batter onto the griddle for each pancake. Wait for bubbles to form and pop, creating small holes in the batter, which takes about 2 to 4 minutes. Flip the pancakes and cook for another 2 minutes until golden brown.

# Ultimate Breakfast Burrito

Prep time: 5 minutes | Cook time: 20 minutes | Serves 2

- 4 eggs
- 4 strips bacon
- 1 large russet potato, peeled and cut into small cubes
- 1 red bell pepper
- ½ yellow onion
- 1 ripe avocado, sliced
- 2 tablespoons hot sauce
- 2 large flour tortillas
- vegetable oil

1. Preheat one side of the griddle to medium-high heat and the other side to medium heat. Brush both sides with vegetable oil. Place the bacon on the medium heat side and the peppers and onions on the medium-high side. Once the bacon is cooked, transfer it to paper towels and chop into small pieces. Add the potatoes to the bacon fat on the griddle and cook until softened. 2. On the vegetable side, crack the eggs and cook them until firm. Once done, assemble the tortillas by layering the cooked ingredients, topping them with avocado slices and a tablespoon of hot sauce. 3. Fold the tortillas and enjoy.

# Crispy Griddle Fried Pickles

Prep time: 10 minutes | Cook time: 10 minutes | Serves 4

- 20 dill pickle slices
- ¼ cup all-purpose flour
- ⅛ teaspoon baking powder
- 3 tablespoons beer or seltzer water
- ⅛ teaspoon sea salt
- 2 tablespoons water, plus more if needed
- 2 tablespoons cornstarch
- 1½ cups panko bread crumbs
- 1 teaspoon paprika
- 1 teaspoon garlic powder
- ¼ teaspoon cayenne pepper
- 2 tablespoons canola oil, divided

1. Preheat the griddle to medium-high heat. 2. Pat the pickle slices dry and place them on a plate in the freezer to chill. 3. In a medium bowl, mix the flour, baking powder, beer, salt, and water until the batter reaches a cake batter consistency. If it's too thick, add more water, 1 teaspoon at a time. 4. Put the cornstarch in a small shallow bowl. 5. In a separate large shallow bowl, mix together the bread crumbs, paprika, garlic powder, and cayenne pepper. 6. Take the pickles out of the freezer and dredge each one in the cornstarch. 7. Shake off any excess, then dip them in the batter, and finally, coat evenly with the bread crumb mixture. 8. Place the breaded pickles on the griddle and gently brush them with 1 tablespoon of oil. Cook for 5 minutes. 9. After 5 minutes, flip the pickles, brush them with the remaining 1 tablespoon of oil, and continue cooking. 10. Once done, serve immediately.

# Steak And Mushroom With Balsamic Sauce

Prep time: 10 minutes | Cook time:20 minutes | Serves 2

- 2 tablespoons butter
- 8 cremini mushrooms, sliced
- 1 tablespoon minced garlic
- 1 teaspoon salt, plus more to taste
- 1 teaspoon pepper, plus more to taste
- Balsamic Griddle Sauce, as needed
- 6-ounce (170g) beef tenderloin fillet, cut in half lengthwise
- 2 prepared crepes
- cooking oil, as needed

1. Melt the butter over medium heat and sauté the mushrooms with the garlic, along with 1 teaspoon each of salt and pepper. 2. The salt will help the mushrooms release their moisture. Once this starts, pour in ¾ cup of the Balsamic Griddle Sauce, cover, and stir occasionally for 6 to 8 minutes. Set the mushrooms aside and keep them warm. 3. Turn the griddle to medium-high heat, and while it heats up, scrape off any residual balsamic sauce to prevent it from burning. 4. Pat the beef dry with paper towels and season generously with salt and pepper. 5. Add oil to the griddle, and when it shimmers, sear the steak for 3 minutes on one side. Flip and sear for another 1 to 3 minutes, depending on how you like it cooked. 6. Let the steak rest for 10 minutes, then slice it thinly against the grain. Serve the steak slices on a crepe and top with the sautéed mushrooms.

# Hearty Denver Skillet Omelet

Prep time: 5 minutes | Cook time: 10 minutes | Serves 2

- 6 large eggs
- ¼ cup country ham, diced
- ¼ cup yellow onion, finely chopped
- ¼ cup green bell pepper, chopped
- ⅔ cup cheddar cheese, shredded
- ¼ teaspoon cayenne pepper
- salt and black pepper
- 2 tablespoons butter

1. Preheat the griddle to medium heat and melt the butter on the surface. 2. Add the ham, onions, and peppers to the butter, cooking until the vegetables have softened slightly. 3. In a large bowl, beat the eggs, then mix in a pinch of salt and cayenne pepper. 4. Divide the cooked vegetables into two portions on the griddle and pour half of the egg mixture over each. Cook until the eggs start to set, then sprinkle cheese over each omelet. 5. Fold the omelets in half and remove them from the griddle. Serve immediately.

# Sausage and Vegetable Scramble

**Prep time: 10 minutes | Cook time: 20 minutes | Serves 4**

- 8 eggs, beaten
- ½ pound (227 g) sausage, sliced into thin rounds or chopped
- 1 green bell pepper, sliced
- 1 yellow onion, sliced
- 1 cup white mushrooms, sliced
- 1 teaspoon salt
- ½ teaspoon black pepper
- vegetable oil

1. Start by setting the griddle to medium-high heat and allow it to warm up. 2. Lightly coat the griddle with vegetable oil and toss on the peppers and mushrooms. 3. Sauté until they begin to turn golden, then add the onions. Season generously with salt and pepper, cooking until the onions become soft and translucent. 4. Add the sausage to the mix and combine it with the vegetables, cooking until the sausage is browned and cooked through. 5. Pour the eggs directly onto the griddle, stir them into the sausage-vegetable mixture, and cook until the eggs are done to your liking. Use a large spatula to scoop up the scramble and serve immediately for a hot, hearty meal.

# Balsamic Steak & Mushroom Crepes

**Prep time: 15 minutes | Cook time: 10 minutes | Serves 4**

- 1 (15-ounce) can full-fat coconut milk, refrigerated overnight
- ½ tablespoon powdered sugar
- 1½ teaspoons vanilla extract, divided
- 1 cup halved strawberries
- 1 tablespoon maple syrup, plus more for garnish
- 1 tablespoon brown sugar, divided
- ¾ cup lite coconut milk
- 2 large eggs
- ½ teaspoon ground cinnamon
- 2 tablespoons unsalted butter, at room temperature
- 4 slices challah bread

1. Flip the chilled can of full-fat coconut milk upside down without shaking it, open the bottom, and pour out the liquid coconut water. Scoop the solid coconut cream into a medium bowl. Use an electric hand mixer to whip the cream for 3 to 5 minutes until soft peaks form. 2. Add the powdered sugar and ½ teaspoon of vanilla extract to the coconut cream and whip again until smooth and creamy. Place the bowl in the refrigerator to chill. 3. Preheat the griddle to medium-high heat. While it preheats, combine the strawberries with maple syrup, tossing to coat evenly. 4. Sprinkle the strawberries with ½ tablespoon of brown sugar. 5. In a large shallow bowl, whisk together the lite coconut milk, eggs, the remaining 1 teaspoon of vanilla, and cinnamon. 6. Place the strawberries on the grill and gently press down to get grill marks. Grill for 4 minutes without flipping. 7. Meanwhile, butter both sides of each bread slice. Dip one slice into the egg mixture, soaking for 1 minute per side. Repeat with the remaining slices, and sprinkle each side with the remaining ½ tablespoon of brown sugar. 8. After 4 minutes, remove the strawberries from the grill and set aside. Lower the heat to medium-low, place the bread on the grill, and cook for 4 to 6 minutes until golden and caramelized, checking often for desired doneness. 9. Transfer the toast to a plate and top with the grilled strawberries and whipped coconut cream. 10. Drizzle with maple syrup, if desired.

# Rustic Egg & Arugula Grilled Pizza

**Prep time: 10 minutes | Cook time: 8 minutes | Serves 2**

- 2 tablespoons all-purpose flour, plus more as needed
- ½ store-bought pizza dough (about 8 ounces / 227 g)
- 1 tablespoon canola oil, divided
- 1 cup fresh ricotta cheese
- 4 large eggs
- Sea salt
- Freshly ground black pepper
- 4 cups arugula, torn
- 1 tablespoon extra-virgin olive oil
- 1 teaspoon freshly squeezed lemon juice
- 2 tablespoons grated Parmesan cheese

1. Begin by preheating the griddle to medium-high heat. 2. Lightly dust a clean surface with flour, then place the dough on it and roll it out to a 9-inch round of even thickness. Be sure to dust your rolling pin and surface with extra flour as needed to prevent sticking. 3. Brush one side of the dough with ½ tablespoon of canola oil, flip it, and brush the other side with the remaining oil. Use a fork to poke 5 or 6 holes across the surface to avoid air pockets while cooking. 4. Lay the dough on the griddle and cook for about 4 minutes. 5. After 4 minutes, flip the dough and evenly dot the surface with small spoonfuls of ricotta cheese, leaving a 1-inch border around the edges. 6. Crack each egg into a small bowl to easily remove any shells and keep the yolk whole. Picture the dough divided into four sections and pour one egg into each section. Repeat for all 4 eggs. Season with salt and pepper. 7. Let the pizza cook for an additional 3 to 4 minutes, until the egg whites are fully set. 8. While the pizza finishes cooking, toss arugula, olive oil, and lemon juice in a medium bowl, seasoning with salt and pepper. Once the pizza is ready, transfer it to a cutting board and let it cool slightly. Top with the arugula mixture, drizzle with olive oil if desired, and sprinkle with Parmesan cheese. 9. Slice the pizza and serve immediately.

# Classic Buttermilk Pancakes

- 2 cups all-purpose flour
- 3 tablespoons sugar
- 1½ teaspoons baking powder
- 1½ teaspoons baking soda
- 1¼ teaspoons salt
- 2½ cups buttermilk
- 2 eggs
- 3 tablespoons unsalted butter, melted
- 2 tablespoons vegetable oil

1. In a large mixing bowl, whisk together the flour, sugar, baking soda, baking powder, and salt until evenly combined. 2. Add the buttermilk, eggs, and melted butter, then gently stir until the ingredients are just combined, leaving some small lumps in the batter. 3. Preheat the griddle to medium heat and lightly coat it with a small amount of oil. Use a paper towel to spread the oil evenly over the surface, creating a very thin layer. 4. Ladle the pancake batter onto the griddle, leaving enough space between each pancake to prevent spreading. 5. Once bubbles form on the surface of the pancakes, flip them and cook for an additional few minutes until both sides are golden brown. Remove the pancakes from the griddle and serve immediately with butter and maple syrup.

# Fluffy Buttermilk Griddle Pancakes

- 2 cups all-purpose flour
- 3 tablespoons sugar
- 2 teaspoons baking powder
- 2 teaspoons baking soda
- pinch kosher salt
- 2 eggs
- 2½ cups buttermilk
- ¼ cup melted butter

1. In a large bowl, sift together the flour, sugar, baking powder, baking soda, and salt until thoroughly combined. 2. In a medium bowl, whisk together the eggs, buttermilk, and melted butter until frothy. Pour this mixture into the dry ingredients and stir until just combined; don't worry about small lumps—it's okay if they remain. Let the batter rest at room temperature for 20 to 30 minutes while your grill preheats. 3. Preheat the griddle to medium-high heat. Lightly oil the surface and let it heat until the oil shimmers without smoking. 4. For each pancake, pour about ¼ cup of batter onto the griddle. Watch as bubbles begin to form slowly on the surface. After 2 to 4 minutes, once the bubbles pop and leave small holes, flip the pancake and cook for an additional 2 minutes until golden brown.

# Classic Lemon-Infused Crepes

- 1 cup all-purpose flour
- 1½ cups milk
- ½ cup water
- 2 eggs
- 1 teaspoon grated lemon
- zest
- 2 pinches salt
- 2 tablespoons melted butter, plus more as needed for the griddle

1. Combine all the ingredients, except the butter, in a blender and blend for 30 to 45 seconds until the batter is smooth. Scrape down the sides if needed, then blend again to ensure everything is well incorporated. Let the batter rest for 30 minutes to allow the ingredients to settle. 2. Preheat the griddle to medium heat. Butter an area about 10 inches wide, then pour ¼ cup of the batter in the center. 3. Use the measuring cup or a crepe spreader to gently spread the batter into a thin, round circle on the griddle. Cook for about 90 seconds, or until the batter is mostly set. Flip the crepe and cook for another 60 to 90 seconds, or until it turns a light golden brown. (You can adjust the doneness to your preference, but cooking them to a yellowish-golden color works well for rolling and stuffing.)

# Golden Hash Browns

- 3 russet potatoes, peeled
- 1 tablespoon onion powder
- 1 tablespoon salt
- 1 teaspoon black pepper
- vegetable oil

1. Grate the potatoes using the largest holes on a box grater and place them in a large bowl. Once all the potatoes are grated, rinse them thoroughly with water. 2. Squeeze out as much excess water as possible from the grated potatoes, then return them to the bowl. 3. Mix in the onion powder, salt, and pepper, stirring until well combined. 4. Preheat your griddle to medium heat and add a generous layer of oil. Spread the potato mixture onto the griddle, forming a layer about ½ inch thick. Cook for approximately 8 minutes. 5. Using a large spatula, work in sections to flip the potatoes and cook for an additional 5 to 8 minutes, or until both sides are golden brown. 6. Carefully remove the potatoes from the griddle in sections and transfer them to plates. Sprinkle with a pinch of salt and serve immediately for a delicious, crispy treat.

# Classic Griddle Diner Omelet

Prep time: 10 minutes | Cook time: 10 minutes | Serves 1

- ½ cup diced red bell pepper
- ½ cup sliced mushrooms
- ½ teaspoon garlic salt
- 2 eggs plus 2 egg yolks
- ½ cup shredded cheddar-
- Jack cheese blend, or 2 slices cheese
- butter, as needed
- salt and pepper, to taste
- cilantro, to serve (optional)

1. Preheat the griddle to medium-low heat. 2. Butter a section of the griddle and gently sauté the peppers and mushrooms. After about 3 minutes, stir the vegetables and sprinkle with garlic salt, then cover to continue cooking. 3. In a medium bowl, beat the eggs until frothy. Using a large spatula, push the pepper and mushroom mixture to one side of the griddle. Melt a generous amount of butter over a large area of the griddle, then slowly pour the eggs onto the cooking surface. Try to shape the eggs into a circle or square using the spatula for easier flipping later. 4. Allow the eggs to cook slowly without much stirring. After about 3 minutes, you'll see bubbles forming as they cook, with some parts firm and others still runny. Evenly distribute the pepper and mushroom mixture over the omelet like you would top a pizza. When about 80 percent of the egg is solidified, sprinkle the cheese evenly on top. 5. Your omelet should have minimal runny or visibly raw egg at this stage. With a long spatula, carefully scrape under the omelet to ensure it releases from the griddle. To fold the omelet, slide the spatula underneath until fully covered, then lift and twist your wrist to fold the omelet in half. 6. Cook for an additional minute, then serve with salt and pepper to taste. Garnish with cilantro if desired.

# Honey-Lime Grilled Fruit Salad

Prep time: 10 minutes | Cook time: 4 minutes | Serves 4

- ½ pound (227 g) strawberries, washed, hulled and halved
- 1 (9 ounces / 255 g) can pineapple chunks, drained, juice reserved
- 2 peaches, pitted and sliced
- 6 tablespoons honey, divided
- 1 tablespoon freshly squeezed lime juice

1. Preheat your griddle to medium-high heat. 2. While the griddle heats up, combine the strawberries, pineapple, and peaches in a large bowl with 3 tablespoons of honey. Toss the fruit to ensure it is evenly coated. 3. Place the fruit on the griddle, pressing down gently to enhance the grill marks. Grill for 4 minutes without flipping. 4. In a small bowl, mix the remaining 3 tablespoons of honey with lime juice and 1 tablespoon of reserved pineapple juice. 5. Once the fruit is done cooking, transfer it to a large bowl and toss it with the honey mixture. Serve immediately for a delicious and refreshing treat!

# Simple French Crepes

Prep time: 1hour | Cook time: 15 minutes | Serves 4

- 1¼ cups flour
- ¾ cup whole milk
- ½ cup water
- 2 eggs
- 3 tablespoons unsalted butter, melted
- 1 teaspoon vanilla
- 2 tablespoons sugar

1. In a large bowl, combine all the ingredients and whisk until the batter is smooth. Let it rest for 1 hour to allow the flavors to meld. 2. Preheat your Blackstone Griddle to medium heat and add a thin layer of butter. Pour about ¼ cup of the batter onto the griddle, using a crepe spreading tool to form a thin, even layer. Cook for 1 to 2 minutes until the edges begin to lift, then use a crepe spatula to flip the crepe. Cook for another minute on the other side. 3. For a sweet crepe, top with Nutella and strawberries, or for a savory option, add scrambled eggs and Black Forest ham. Enjoy!

# Savory Chicken Bacon & Artichoke Crepes

Prep time: 10 minutes | Cook time:15 minutes | Serves 2

- 4 slices bacon
- 8 ounces (227g) chicken breast, cut into small cubes
- White Wine Griddle Sauce
- 3 marinated artichoke
- hearts, quartered
- 2 prepared crepes
- ⅓ cup ranch dressing
- salt and pepper, to taste

1. Preheat the griddle to medium-high heat and cook the bacon until crispy. Remove the bacon and set it aside to keep warm. 2. In the leftover bacon fat, add the cubed chicken, seasoning with salt and pepper. Sauté for about 4 minutes without moving the chicken too much, allowing it to brown nicely. Add the White Wine Griddle Sauce as needed, cover, and cook for an additional 4 to 6 minutes until the chicken is fully cooked. Remove the chicken and keep it warm. 3. In the remaining bits on the griddle, sauté the marinated artichokes for 3 to 5 minutes until they're heated through and slightly browned. 4. Spread half of the ranch dressing on each crepe, then fill the crepes with the chicken, bacon, and artichoke pieces. Serve immediately.

# Bacon Egg and Cheese Sandwich

- ♦ 4 large eggs
- ♦ 8 strips of bacon
- ♦ 4 slices cheddar or American cheese
- ♦ 8 slices sourdough bread
- ♦ 2 tablespoons butter
- ♦ 2 tablespoons vegetable oil

1. Preheat your griddle to medium heat and lay the strips of bacon on one side. Cook until they are slightly crispy. 2. When the bacon is nearly done, pour oil onto the other side of the griddle and crack the eggs onto the surface. Cook them sunny side up or over medium, depending on your preference. 3. Butter one side of each slice of bread and place them butter side down on the griddle. Top 4 of the slices with a slice of cheese, and once the cheese starts to melt and the eggs are done, stack the eggs on the bread. 4. Add the cooked bacon to the sandwiches and place the remaining slices of bread on top. Serve immediately for a delicious breakfast treat.

# Pepper Ring Eggs Belledict

- ♦ 1 medium red or green bell pepper
- ♦ 2 English muffins
- ♦ 2 eggs
- ♦ 4 slices Canadian bacon
- ♦ ½ cup very finely shredded Jarlsberg cheese
- ♦ butter, as needed

1. Preheat the griddle to medium heat. Cut off the uneven bottom of the bell pepper, then slice two rings about ½ inch thick. 2. Generously coat the griddle with butter. Separate the English muffins and place the cut sides down on the griddle to warm up. Add the bell pepper rings and cook for 2 minutes. Flip the peppers, then turn the English muffins to heat the other sides. 3. Crack an egg and gently drop it into one of the bell pepper rings. Position the second pepper ring nearby and repeat with the second egg. Cover the eggs with a lid slightly larger than the peppers and let them cook for 1 minute. 4. While the eggs are cooking, warm the Canadian bacon on the griddle. 5. Remove the lid from the eggs and carefully squirt some water around the grilling surface near the eggs. Immediately cover the eggs again to trap the steam, which will help cook the whites and yolks. Cook for another minute, then sprinkle half of the cheese over each egg. The finer the cheese is grated, the quicker it will melt, so using a very fine grater or Microplane works well. Squirt water around the eggs again and cover to allow the cheese to melt. 6. Take the English muffins off the griddle and place 2 slices of Canadian bacon on each half. Uncover the eggs, and with a spatula, carefully lift the pepper ring containing the egg and slide it onto the Canadian bacon. Top with the other half of the English muffin.

# Spicy Bacon Potato Hash

- ♦ 6 slices thick cut bacon
- ♦ 2 russet potatoes, cut into ½ inch chunks
- ♦ 1 yellow onion, chopped
- ♦ 1 red bell pepper, chopped
- ♦ 1 clove garlic, finely chopped
- ♦ 1 teaspoon salt
- ♦ ½ teaspoon black pepper
- ♦ 1 tablespoon Tabasco sauce

1. Preheat your griddle to medium heat and cook the bacon until it's just crispy. 2. Add the diced potato, onion, and bell pepper to the griddle, cooking until the potato is softened. Spread the ingredients out over the large surface of the griddle for even cooking. 3. Once the potatoes are tender, stir in the garlic, salt, and pepper. 4. Chop the cooked bacon into small pieces and mix it into the griddle. Stir the mixture well and add hot sauce just before removing the hash from the griddle. Serve immediately for a delicious meal!

# Bacon and Gruyere Omelet

- ♦ 6 eggs, beaten
- ♦ 6 strips bacon
- ♦ ¼ pound (113 g) gruyere, shredded
- ♦ 1 teaspoon black pepper
- ♦ 1 teaspoon salt
- ♦ 1 tablespoon chives, finely chopped
- ♦ vegetable oil

1. Season the beaten eggs with salt and let them sit for 10 minutes. 2. Preheat your griddle to medium heat and add the bacon strips. Cook until most of the fat has rendered, but the bacon remains flexible. Remove the bacon from the griddle and place it on paper towels to drain. 3. Once the bacon has drained, chop it into small pieces. 4. Pour the eggs onto the griddle in two even pools. Cook until the bottom of the eggs starts to firm up. Sprinkle the gruyere cheese over the eggs and continue cooking until the cheese begins to melt and the eggs are lightly browned. 5. Add the chopped bacon to the eggs, then use a spatula to fold one half of the omelet over the other. 6. Remove the omelet from the griddle, season with pepper and chives, and serve immediately.

# Cheesy Bacon Hash Brown Scramble

**Prep time: 10 minutes | Cook time: 10 minutes | Serves 4**

- 2 russet potatoes, shredded, rinsed, and drained
- 8 eggs, beaten
- 1 cup cheddar cheese
- 6 slices bacon, cut into small pieces
- ⅓ cup green onion, chopped
- vegetable oil

1. Preheat the griddle to medium heat and lightly brush it with vegetable oil. 2. Spread the grated potatoes on one side of the griddle, forming a layer about ½ inch thick. Cook until they are golden brown, then flip. On the other side of the griddle, add the bacon and cook until the fat has rendered and the bacon is crispy. 3. Top the hash browns with the eggs and cheese, then mix in the cooked bacon and green onions. Cook until the cheese has melted, then divide the mixture equally among 4 plates.

# Chorizo Breakfast Tacos

**Prep time: 10 minutes | Cook time: 10 minutes | Serves 3**

- 4 eggs
- ¼ cup milk
- ½ pound (227g) chorizo
- butter, as needed
- ½ cup chopped green pepper
- ½ cup diced sweet onion
- 6 corn tortillas
- ½ cup shredded cheddar cheese
- cooking oil, as needed

1. Crack the eggs into a medium bowl and whisk them together with the milk until fully combined. 2. Preheat the griddle to medium-high heat. 3. Once the grill is hot, add the chorizo to cook. Use a stiff spatula or metal scraper to continually chop the chorizo as it cooks, ensuring even browning and breaking it into small pieces. Cover the chorizo to allow it to cook completely. 4. While the chorizo cooks, melt a few pats of butter on the griddle and sauté the peppers and onions until the peppers are wilted and the onions are translucent. Mix the cooked chorizo with the sautéed vegetables, spreading them evenly on the griddle. 5. If necessary, add more butter to ensure the griddle is well-greased before pouring the egg mixture over the chorizo and veggies. Use a wide spatula or scraper to stir the mixture as it cooks, allowing the eggs to form curds. As the eggs solidify, scrape them, along with the chorizo and veggies, to the side and cover to keep warm. 6. Lightly coat the griddle with oil and let it heat until shimmering. Place the tortillas in the oil and cook for about 2 minutes on each side until slightly

crisp. 7. Uncover the chorizo mixture and sprinkle cheese on top. Cook until the cheese has melted. 8. To assemble the tacos, divide the chorizo mixture into thirds and scoop it into a double-layered tortilla, topping it with the melted cheese.

# Mexican Scramble

**Prep time: 5 minutes | Cook time: 10 minutes | Serves 4**

- 8 eggs, beaten
- 1 pound (454 g) Chorizo
- ½ yellow onion
- 1 cup cooked black beans
- ½ cup green chilies
- ½ cup jack cheese
- ¼ cup green onion, chopped
- ½ teaspoon black pepper
- vegetable oil

1. Set the griddle to medium heat and allow it to preheat. Lightly brush the surface with vegetable oil. Place the chorizo on one side of the griddle and the onions on the other. Once the onions have softened, mix them with the chorizo. Stir in the beans and chilies, letting everything heat through. Add the eggs, cheese, and green onion, cooking until the eggs are done to your preferred firmness. 2. Transfer the scramble from the griddle, sprinkle with black pepper, and serve immediately for a flavorful, hearty dish.

# Fluffy Blueberry Pancakes

**Prep time: 10 minutes | Cook time: 10 minutes | Serves 2**

- 1 cup flour
- ¾ cup milk
- 2 tablespoons white vinegar
- 2 tablespoons sugar
- 1 teaspoon baking powder
- ½ teaspoon baking soda
- ½ teaspoon salt
- 1 egg
- 2 tablespoons butter, melted
- 1 cup fresh blueberries
- butter for cooking

1. In a small bowl, mix the milk and vinegar, then set it aside for two minutes to thicken. 2. In a large mixing bowl, combine the flour, sugar, baking powder, baking soda, and salt. Add the milk mixture, egg, blueberries, and melted butter. Stir until just combined, leaving a few small lumps. 3. Preheat the griddle to medium heat and melt a bit of butter on the surface. Pour the pancake batter onto the griddle, cooking until bubbles form and the edges are golden brown. 4. Flip the pancakes and cook until the other side is also golden. 5. Remove the pancakes from the griddle and serve immediately with warm maple syrup.

# Classic Steak and Eggs

- 1 pound (454 g) Sirloin, cut into 4 ½-inch thick pieces
- 8 large eggs
- 3 tablespoons vegetable oil
- salt and black pepper

1. Preheat the griddle to medium-high heat on one side and medium heat on the other. 2. Generously season the steaks with salt and pepper. 3. Place the steaks on the medium-high side of the griddle and cook for 3 minutes. Then, add oil to the medium heat side. 4. Flip the steaks and crack the eggs onto the medium heat side of the griddle. 5. After another 3 minutes, remove the steaks from the griddle and let them rest for 5 minutes. Finish cooking the eggs, then plate two eggs alongside one steak on each plate. Season the eggs with a pinch of salt and pepper before serving.

# Vanilla Ice Cream French Toast Delight

- 1 cup melted vanilla ice cream
- 3 eggs
- 1 teaspoon vanilla extract
- pinch of ground cinnamon
- 8 slices Texas toast or other thick-cut bread
- cooking oil, as needed

1. In a bowl wide enough for easy dipping, combine the melted ice cream, eggs, vanilla extract, and cinnamon. Mix thoroughly until the mixture is frothy. 2. Preheat the griddle to medium-high heat and coat the surface with oil. Once the oil begins to shimmer, dip each slice of bread into the egg mixture, ensuring both sides are lightly coated. Let any excess batter drain back into the bowl. 3. Place the coated bread on the griddle and cook for 3 to 4 minutes per side, or until the French toast is a beautiful golden brown. Continue this process with the remaining bread slices.

# Potato Pancakes

- 2 eggs
- ¼ cup milk
- 1½ cups russet potato, peeled and shredded
- ¼ cup all-purpose flour
- ¼ cup finely diced onion
- ¼ cup finely chopped green onion
- 1 teaspoon baking powder
- 1 teaspoon salt
- 1 teaspoon pepper
- cooking oil, as needed

1. In a large bowl, whisk the eggs and milk together until frothy. Incorporate the remaining ingredients and mix until well combined. The batter should be moist but not overly liquidy. Let it rest for 20 minutes while the grill heats up. 2. Preheat the griddle to medium-high heat. 3. Apply a thin layer of oil to the cooking surface. Once the oil starts to shimmer, pour about ¼ cup of the potato pancake batter onto the griddle for each pancake. Use a spatula to press the batter down slightly, and cook each side for 3 to 4 minutes, or until they are golden brown.

# Chapter 2

# Pizzas, Wraps, and Sandwiches

# Chapter 2 Pizzas, Wraps, and Sandwiches

## Southwest Spiced Turkey Burgers

**Prep time: 10 minutes | Cook time: 15 minutes | Serves 4**

- ⅓ cup finely crushed corn tortilla chips
- 1 egg, beaten
- ¼ cup salsa
- ⅓ cup shredded pepper Jack cheese
- Pinch salt
- Freshly ground black pepper
- 1 pound (454 g) ground turkey
- 1 tablespoon olive oil
- 1 teaspoon paprika

1. In a medium bowl, combine the tortilla chips, egg, salsa, cheese, salt, and pepper, mixing thoroughly. 2. Gently fold in the turkey using clean hands, ensuring everything is well incorporated. 3. Shape the mixture into patties about ½ inch thick, making a slight indentation in the center of each patty with your thumb to prevent them from puffing up while cooking. 4. Brush both sides of the patties with olive oil and sprinkle paprika over them. 5. Preheat the griddle by turning the control knob to high. Once hot, cook the patties for 14 to 16 minutes, or until the internal temperature reaches at least 165°F.

## Garlic Parmesan Griddle Cheese Sandwiches

**Prep time: 2 minutes | Cook time: 7 minutes | Serves 1**

- 2 slices Italian bread, sliced thin
- 2 slices provolone cheese
- 2 tablespoons butter, softened
- Garlic powder, for dusting
- Dried parsley, for dusting
- Parmesan Cheese, shredded, for dusting

1. Generously spread butter on 2 slices of bread, then evenly sprinkle garlic and parsley over each buttered side. 2. Add a few tablespoons of Parmesan cheese on top of the butter, gently pressing it into the bread for better adherence. 3. Preheat the griddle to medium heat and place one slice of bread, buttered side down, onto the hot surface. 4. Layer provolone slices over the bread, then place the second slice of bread on top, buttered side facing up. 5. Cook for 3 minutes before carefully flipping the sandwich to cook for another 3 minutes on the opposite side, until the bread is golden brown and the Parmesan is crispy. 6. Enjoy your deliciously crispy grilled cheese warm, accompanied by your favorite sides for a perfect meal!

## Chipotle Burgers With Avocado

**Prep time: 5 minutes | Cook time: 5 minutes | Serves 4**

- 1¼ pounds (567 g) lean ground beef
- 2 tablespoons chipotle puree
- ½ teaspoon salt
- ¼ teaspoon freshly ground black pepper
- slices cheddar cheese (about 4 ounces / 113 g)
- 1 avocado, halved, pitted, and sliced
- ¼ head iceberg lettuce, shredded
- 4 hamburger buns, toasted

1. In a medium bowl, combine the ground beef with the chipotle purée, salt, and pepper. Use a fork to mix the seasonings into the meat, then use your hands to form the mixture into 4 patties, each approximately 1 inch thick. 2. Preheat the griddle by turning the control knob to the high position. Once the griddle is hot, place the burgers on it and cook for 4 minutes without flipping. After 4 minutes, top each burger with a slice of cheese and cook for an additional minute until the cheese is melted. Remove the burgers from the griddle and cover them to keep warm. 3. Assemble each burger by topping with a few slices of avocado and some shredded lettuce, then sandwich between a bun. 4. For the chipotle purée, blend canned chipotles with their liquid in a blender or food processor until smooth. 5. The purée can be covered with plastic wrap and refrigerated for up to 2 weeks. Use it sparingly, as it packs a spicy punch! I recommend incorporating it into meat marinades and dips. You can also find this purée in some grocery stores or ethnic markets.

# Crispy Griddle Pastrami Reuben

**Prep time: 5 minutes | Cook time:10 minutes | Serves 1**

- 4 slices deli pastrami
- 1 tablespoon Dijon mustard
- 3 tablespoons Thousand Island dressing
- 2 slices rye bread
- 4 slices Swiss cheese
- 2 tablespoons mayonnaise

1. Preheat the griddle to medium heat. 2. Place the sliced pastrami on the grill and cook for 3 to 5 minutes, turning frequently until the slices start to brown and shrink. Generously coat the cooked pastrami with Dijon mustard and set it aside. 3. To assemble the sandwich, spread Thousand Island dressing on each slice of bread. Next, place two slices of Swiss cheese on each bread slice, letting about ¾ inch hang over the edge. Add the pastrami to the sandwich, spread a layer of mayonnaise on top, and close the sandwich. 4. Grill the sandwich, covered, over medium heat for 3 to 4 minutes on each side, allowing the Swiss cheese to melt and become crispy on the griddle. Be cautious when flipping or removing the sandwich; use a spatula to carefully scrape underneath the melted cheese to maintain its shape.

# Pineapple Teriyaki Turkey Burgers

**Prep time: 5 minutes | Cook time: 9 minutes | Serves 4**

- 1 teaspoon BBQ rub
- 1 can sliced pineapple
- 4 slices Swiss cheese

patry:

- 1 pound (454 g) ground turkey
- ½ cup bread crumbs
- ¼ cup teriyaki sauce
- 1 small yellow onion, diced
- 1 cup fresh raw spinach, stems removed
- 4 sets of hamburger buns

- 2 tablespoons finely chopped parsley
- 2 cloves garlic, minced
- 1 egg, beaten

1. In a large mixing bowl, thoroughly combine all the ingredients for the patties, mixing by hand until well blended. 2. Divide the mixture into four equal portions and shape each portion into a patty. Place the patties on a sheet of parchment paper and evenly sprinkle each one with BBQ rub. Refrigerate for 30 minutes to firm up. 3. Preheat the griddle to high heat. Once hot, add the burgers along with the pineapple slices. Cook for 4 minutes without flipping. After this time, remove the burgers and cover them to keep warm. 4. Flip the burgers over and place a slice of Swiss cheese on each patty, allowing it to melt as the patties finish cooking. Once melted, remove from the griddle. 5. Assemble the burgers on buns, layering with fresh spinach and the grilled pineapple slices for added flavor.

# Spiced Lamb Burger

**Prep time: 5 minutes | Cook time: 5 minutes | Serves 4**

- 1¼ pounds (567 g) lean ground lamb
- tablespoon ground cumin
- ¼ teaspoon ground cinnamon
- ½ teaspoon salt
- ½ teaspoon freshly ground black pepper
- whole wheat pitas
- ½ medium cucumber, peeled and sliced
- ½ cup Simple Garlic Yogurt Sauce

1. In a medium bowl, combine the lamb with cumin, cinnamon, salt, and pepper. Use a fork to thoroughly mix the seasonings into the meat, then shape the mixture into 4 patties, each approximately 1 inch thick, using your hands. 2. Set the griddle control knob to high. Once the griddle is hot, place the patties on it and cook for 5 minutes without flipping. After cooking, remove the burgers and cover them to keep warm. 3. To assemble, place a burger inside each pita pocket, add a few cucumber slices, and generously spoon yogurt sauce on top. Serve right away for a delicious meal!

# Grilled Pizza Cheese

**Prep time: 10 minutes | Cook time: 20 minutes | Serves 4**

- 8 slices French bread
- 3 tablespoons butter, softened
- ½ cup pizza sauce
- ¼ cup mozzarella cheese
- ½ cup pepperoni diced
- Garlic powder, for dusting
- Oregano, for dusting

1. Generously butter one side of each slice of French bread. 2. Position the slices butter-side down on a sheet of aluminum foil and sprinkle with garlic powder and oregano for extra flavor. 3. On the unbuttered side of each slice, spread a layer of pizza sauce evenly. 4. Take 4 of the slices and top them with a layer of mozzarella cheese, followed by a few pepperoni slices, and then add another layer of mozzarella on top. 5. Place the remaining slices on top of the prepared ones, ensuring the buttered sides face up, to form 4 delicious sandwiches. 6. Heat the griddle to medium heat and carefully place one sandwich, buttered side down, onto it. 7. Cook for 3 minutes, then flip to cook the other side for an additional 3 minutes, until the bread is golden brown and the cheese is perfectly melted. 8. Serve the sandwiches warm and savor every bite!

# Roasted Green Chile Salsa Verde

Prep time: 5 minutes | Cook time: 15 minutes | Serves 1 cup

- cloves garlic (leave the skins on),
- skewered on a wooden toothpick or small bamboo skewer
- 1 cup roasted New Mexican green chiles or Anaheim chiles cut into ¼-inch strips (8 to 10 chiles
- 2 tablespoons chopped fresh
- cilantro
- 2 teaspoons fresh lime juice, or more to
- taste
- ½ teaspoon ground cumin
- ½ teaspoon dried oregano
- Coarse salt (kosher or sea) and freshly
- ground black pepper

1. Preheat the griddle to high heat. Once it's hot, lightly oil the griddle surface and place the burgers on it. Cook the burgers for 4 to 6 minutes. In the meantime, add the garlic cloves to the griddle and cook until they are lightly browned and tender, about 2 to 3 minutes per side (totaling 4 to 6 minutes). If any garlic skin gets too burnt, scrape it off. In a blender, combine the cooked garlic, chile strips, cilantro, lime juice, cumin, oregano, and 4 tablespoons of water. Purée until smooth, scraping down the sides of the blender with a spatula as needed. 2. Transfer the salsa mixture to a saucepan and bring it to a gentle simmer over medium heat. Allow it to simmer for 5 to 8 minutes, stirring occasionally with a wooden spoon, until it thickens and becomes flavorful. The salsa should reach a consistency similar to heavy cream but remain pourable; add more water if necessary. Taste for seasoning, adjusting with additional lime juice, salt, and pepper to ensure a robust flavor.

# Pork Tenderloin Sandwiches

Prep time: 10 minutes | Cook time: 25 minutes | Serves 6

- 2 (¾ pounds /340 g) pork tenderloins
- teaspoon garlic powder
- 1 teaspoon sea salt
- 1 teaspoon dry mustard
- ½ teaspoon coarsely ground pepper
- Olive oil, for brushing
- whole wheat hamburger buns
- tablespoons barbecue sauce

1. In a small mixing bowl, combine garlic, salt, pepper, and mustard, stirring well to create a seasoning blend. 2. Rub the pork tenderloins generously with olive oil, followed by the seasoning mixture to coat them evenly. 3. Preheat the griddle to medium-high heat and cook the pork for 10 to 12 minutes on each side, or until a meat thermometer inserted into the thickest part reads 155°F. 4.

Once cooked, remove the tenderloins from the griddle and let them rest for 10 minutes to allow the juices to settle. 5. After resting, slice the pork thinly and distribute the slices evenly onto hamburger buns. 6. Drizzle barbecue sauce over each sandwich for added flavor and serve immediately.

# Griddle Pizza Cheese

Prep time: 10 minutes | Cook time: 20 minutes | Serves 4

- 8 slices French bread
- 3 tablespoons butter, softened
- ½ cup pizza sauce
- ¼ cup mozzarella cheese
- ½ cup pepperoni diced
- Garlic powder, for dusting
- Oregano, for dusting

1. Generously butter one side of each slice of French bread. 2. Position the slices butter-side down on a sheet of aluminum foil and sprinkle with garlic powder and oregano for added flavor. 3. On the unbuttered side of each slice, spread a layer of pizza sauce evenly. 4. Take 4 of the slices and top them with mozzarella cheese, followed by a few pepperoni slices, and finish with more mozzarella. 5. Place the remaining slices on top of the prepared ones, ensuring the buttered sides face up, to form 4 delicious sandwiches. 6. Heat the griddle to medium heat and carefully place one sandwich, buttered side down, onto it. 7. Cook for 3 minutes, then flip to cook the other side for an additional 3 minutes, until the bread turns golden brown and the cheese has melted. 8. Serve the sandwiches warm and savor the flavors!

# Creamy Bacon Jalapeño Poppers

Prep time: 5 minutes | Cook time: 10 minutes | Serves 4

- package bacon, uncured and nitrate free
- fresh jalapeno peppers, halved lengthwise and
- seeded
- 1 (8 ounce) package cream cheese
- 1 dozen toothpicks, soaked

1. Begin by preheating your griddle to a high temperature. 2. Generously fill the halved jalapeños with cream cheese until they are well-stuffed. 3. Carefully wrap each filled jalapeño with a slice of bacon and secure it in place with a toothpick. 4. Arrange the wrapped jalapeños on the griddle and cook until the bacon becomes crispy, which should take about 5 to 7 minutes on each side. 5. Once done, transfer the jalapeño poppers to a platter and let them cool slightly before serving them warm.

# Classic Big Griddle Burger

**Prep time: 5 minutes | Cook time: 9 minutes | Serves 4**

- 1¼ pounds (567 g) lean ground beef
- ½ teaspoon salt
- ½ teaspoon freshly ground black pepper
- Seasoning of your choice (such as a dash of Worcestershire or hot sauce, or 1 teaspoon Spicy Spanish Rub

- 4 slices cheese such as American, cheddar, or Swiss (about 4 ounces / 113 g), or ¼ cup
- crumbled blue or goat cheese
- 4 toasted buns
- 4 beefsteak tomato slices
- 4 leaves romaine lettuce

1. Preheat the griddle to medium-high heat. In a medium bowl, combine the ground beef with salt, pepper, and any other seasonings you like. 2. Use a fork to thoroughly mix the seasonings into the meat, then shape the mixture into four patties, each roughly 1 inch thick. Once the griddle is hot, place the burgers on it and cook for 4 minutes without flipping them. 3. The burgers are done when the internal temperature reaches at least 145°F, as measured with a food thermometer. If necessary, continue cooking for an additional 5 minutes. 4. Once cooked, place a slice of cheese on top of each burger and lower the griddle lid. Allow the cheese to melt for about 30 seconds. 5. Assemble the burgers by placing them on the bottom halves of the buns, adding a slice of tomato and a crisp lettuce leaf to each one, and topping with the other half of the bun. Serve right away!

# Gourmet Grilled Salmon Burgers

**Prep time: 5 minutes | Cook time: 11 minutes | Serves 4**

- 1½ pounds (680 g) salmon fillet, skin and any remaining pin bones removed, cut into chunks
- 2 teaspoons Dijon mustard
- 3 scallions, trimmed and chopped
- ¼ cup bread crumbs (preferably fresh)

- Salt and pepper
- Good-quality olive oil for brushing
- sesame hamburger buns or 8–10 slider buns (like potato or dinner rolls)
- 1 large tomato, cut into 4 thick slices

1. In a food processor, combine about a quarter of the salmon with the mustard and purée into a smooth paste. Add the remaining salmon and pulse until chopped but still chunky. Transfer the mixture to a bowl, then mix in the scallions, bread crumbs, and a sprinkle of salt and pepper. Gently combine the ingredients just enough to mix. Form the mixture into 4 burgers that are ¾ to 1 inch thick. Place the patties on a plate, cover with plastic wrap, and chill in the refrigerator until firm, for at least 2 hours or up to 8 hours. 2. Preheat your griddle by turning the control knob to the high position. Once the griddle is hot, brush both sides of the burgers with oil and place them on the griddle. Cook for 11 minutes. 3. After 11 minutes, check the burgers for doneness. They are ready when the internal temperature reaches at least 165°F as measured by a food thermometer. 4. If they need more time, close the griddle hood and continue cooking for up to 2 additional minutes. 5. Once cooked, remove the burgers from the griddle. Place the buns cut side down on the griddle and toast for 1 to 2 minutes until golden brown. Serve the burgers on the toasted buns, adding tomato slices if desired.

# Zesty Basil–Ginger Shrimp Sliders

**Prep time: 5 minutes | Cook time: 10 minutes | Serves 4**

- large clove garlic, peeled
- 1 1-inch piece fresh ginger, peeled and
- sliced
- 1½ pounds (680 g) shrimp, peeled (and deveined if you like)
- ½ cup lightly packed fresh basil leaves
- ¼ cup roughly chopped shallots, scallions, or red

- onion
- Salt and pepper
- Sesame oil for brushing the burgers
- sesame hamburger buns or 8–10 slider buns
- Lime wedges for serving
- Lettuce, sliced tomato, and other
- condiments for serving (optional)

1. In a food processor, combine garlic, ginger, and one-third of the shrimp. Purée until smooth, stopping occasionally to scrape down the sides. Add the remaining shrimp, along with basil and shallots, and season with salt and pepper. Pulse to chop the mixture. Shape it into 4 burgers, each about ¾ inch thick, or 8 to 10 sliders if preferred. Transfer the burgers to a plate, cover with plastic wrap, and refrigerate until firm, which can take at least 1 hour or up to 8 hours. 2. Set the griddle control knob to high. Once hot, brush both sides of the burgers with oil and place them on the griddle. Cook until the bottoms are browned and they release easily, about 5 to 7 minutes. Carefully flip the burgers and cook until they are opaque throughout, about 3 to 5 minutes more. 3. While the burgers are cooking, place the buns cut side down on the griddle to toast. Serve the cooked burgers on the toasted buns with lime wedges, either plain or dressed to your liking.

# Griddle Vegetable Pizza

- 8 small fresh mushrooms, halved
- 1 small zucchini, cut into ¼-inch slices
- 1 small yellow pepper, sliced
- 1 small red pepper, sliced
- 1 small red onion, sliced
- 1 tablespoon white wine vinegar
- 1 tablespoon water
- 4 teaspoons olive oil,

- divided
- ½ teaspoon dried basil
- ¼ teaspoon sea salt
- ¼ teaspoon pepper
- 1 prebaked, 12-inch thin whole wheat pizza crust
- 1 can (8 ounces / 227 g) pizza sauce
- 1 small tomatoes, chopped
- 2 cups shredded part-skim mozzarella cheese

1. Begin by preheating your griddle to medium-high heat. 2. In a large mixing bowl, combine the mushrooms, zucchini, peppers, onion, vinegar, water, 3 teaspoons of oil, and seasonings. 3. Transfer the mixture to the griddle and cook over medium heat for about 10 minutes, stirring frequently, until the vegetables are tender. 4. Brush the pizza crust with the remaining oil and spread pizza sauce evenly over the top. 5. Layer the cooked griddle vegetables, sliced tomatoes, and cheese on top of the sauce. 6. Tent the pizza with aluminum foil and griddle over medium heat for 5 to 7 minutes, or until the edges are lightly browned and the cheese is melted. 7. Serve warm for a delicious meal!

# Zesty Horseradish Brunch Burgers

- ¼ cup light sour cream
- 5 tablespoons white horseradish
- ¼ teaspoon salt
- 1¼ pounds (567 g) lean ground beef
- ¼ cup tomato sauce
- 2 tablespoons Worcestershire sauce

- A dash or 2 of hot sauce
- 1 teaspoon celery salt
- 4 beefsteak tomato slices
- 4 brioche buns or hamburger buns,
- toasted
- 2 celery stalks, with leafy greens, each cut into 4 pieces

1. In a small bowl, mix together the sour cream, 2 tablespoons of horseradish, and salt until well combined. 2. In a medium bowl, combine the ground beef with the remaining 3 tablespoons of horseradish, tomato sauce, Worcestershire sauce, hot sauce, and celery salt. 3. Using a fork, thoroughly mix the seasonings into the meat, then use your hands to form the mixture into 4 patties, each about 1 inch thick. 4. Preheat the griddle by turning the control knob to the high position. Once the griddle is hot, place the patties on it and cook for 4 minutes without flipping. After cooking, remove the burgers from the griddle and cover them to keep warm. 5. Top each burger with a tablespoon of the horseradish sour cream and a slice of tomato, then sandwich between toasted buns. Serve immediately with celery sticks on the side for a refreshing crunch!

# Mediterranean Veggie Pesto Flatbread

- 2 flatbreads
- jar pesto
- cup shredded mozzarella cheese
- For the topping:
- ½ cup cherry tomatoes, halved
- 1 small red onion, sliced thin

- 1 red bell pepper, sliced
- 1 yellow bell pepper, sliced
- ½ cup mixed black and green olives, halved
- 1 small yellow squash or zucchini, sliced
- teaspoon olive oil
- ¼ teaspoon sea salt
- ¼ teaspoon black pepper

1. Begin by preheating the griddle to a low temperature. 2. Evenly spread pesto over each flatbread, ensuring full coverage. 3. Add ½ cup of mozzarella cheese on top of each flatbread. 4. In a large mixing bowl, combine all the topping ingredients and mix them well using a rubber spatula. 5. Arrange the flatbreads on the griddle, distributing the topping mixture evenly over each one, and spread it all the way to the edges. 6. Cover the flatbreads with aluminum foil to create a tent, allowing them to cook for 5 minutes or until the cheese has just melted. 7. Once done, transfer the flatbreads to a cutting board or flat surface and slice each one using a pizza cutter or kitchen scissors. 8. Serve while warm and enjoy the delicious flavors!

# Balsamic Marinated Portobello Sliders

Prep time: 15 minutes | Cook time: 15 minutes | Serves 4

- portobello mushroom caps
- slices mozzarella cheese
- 4 buns, like brioche
- For the marinade:
- ¼ cup balsamic vinegar
- 2 tablespoons olive oil
- teaspoon dried basil
- 1 teaspoon dried oregano
- 1 teaspoon garlic powder
- ¼ teaspoon sea salt
- ¼ teaspoon black pepper

1. In a large mixing bowl, whisk together the marinade ingredients until well combined. Add the mushroom caps and toss them to ensure they are evenly coated. 2. Allow the mushrooms to marinate at room temperature for 15 minutes, turning them twice to absorb the flavors. 3. Preheat the griddle to medium-high heat. 4. Place the marinated mushrooms on the griddle, reserving the marinade for basting later. 5. Cook the mushrooms for 5 to 8 minutes on each side, or until they become tender. 6. Brush the mushrooms with the reserved marinade frequently as they cook. 7. During the last 2 minutes of cooking, top the mushrooms with mozzarella cheese and let it melt. 8. Once done, remove the mushrooms from the griddle and serve them on toasted brioche buns for a delicious meal!

# Turkey Burger

Prep time: 5 minutes | Cook time: 4 minutes | Serves 4

- 1 pound (454 g)ground turkey
- cup pine nuts or walnut pieces
- tablespoons grated Parmesan cheese
- tablespoons store-bought pesto
- ¼ teaspoon salt
- ¼ teaspoon freshly ground black pepper
- whole wheat pitas
- romaine lettuce leaves or 1 small handful arugula
- Lemon

1. Heat the griddle to a high temperature. 2. In a medium-sized bowl, combine the ground turkey with the pine nuts, Parmesan cheese, pesto, salt, and pepper. Use a fork to thoroughly blend the ingredients into the meat, then use your hands to shape the mixture into four patties, each approximately 1 inch thick. 3. Place the patties on the griddle and cook for about 4 minutes, or until they are nicely marked by the griddle and fully cooked. Once done, place each burger inside a pita pocket filled with fresh lettuce and a splash of lemon juice. Serve hot and enjoy!

# Classic American Burger

Prep time: 15 minutes | Cook time: 35 minutes | Serves 6

- 2 pounds (907 g). ground beef, at least 20% fat
- kosher salt
- black pepper
- 1 tomato, sliced
- 1 yellow or red onion, sliced
- 1 head iceberg lettuce, cut into flats
- 6 thick pieces of American or medium cheddar cheese
- 6 seeded buns or potato buns, toasted

1. Begin by dividing the ground beef into 6 equal portions and gently shape each portion into a loosely formed ball. Flatten the balls on a flat surface to create patties, being careful not to overwork the meat. 2. Generously season both sides of the patties with salt and freshly ground black pepper. 3. Preheat your griddle to medium-high heat. 4. Place the patties on the griddle and press down lightly to ensure good contact with the cooking surface. Cook for about three to four minutes. 5. Flip the patties and add a slice of cheese on top of each. Continue cooking for another three to four minutes, allowing the cheese to melt. 6. Once cooked, remove the burgers from the griddle and place them on buns. Top with fresh lettuce, sliced tomato, onion, and your favorite condiments for a delicious finish!

# Chapter 3 Beef, Pork, and Lamb

## Beef Skewers

| Prep time: 10 minutes | Cook time: 15 minutes | Serves 4 |
| --- | --- | --- |

- 1 pound (454 g) beef sirloin tips
- 1 zucchini, cut into chunks

For marinade:
- ¼ cup olive oil
- 1 jalapeno pepper
- ½ tablespoon lime juice
- 1½ tablespoon red wine
- vinegar
- 1 teaspoon dried oregano
- 2 garlic cloves
- 1 cup cilantro

1. Combine all marinade ingredients in a blender and blend until smooth. 2. Transfer the blended marinade into a mixing bowl, add the beef tips, and mix thoroughly to ensure the meat is well coated. Allow it to marinate for 30 minutes for optimal flavor. 3. Thread the marinated beef tips and zucchini chunks onto skewers, alternating between the two. 4. Preheat the griddle to high heat. 5. Lightly spray the griddle surface with cooking spray to prevent sticking. 6. Place the skewers on the hot griddle and cook for 7 to 8 minutes, turning occasionally, or until the beef tips are cooked to your desired doneness. 7. Once cooked, serve the skewers hot and enjoy your meal!

## Citrus-Basted Cuban Pork Chops

| Prep time: 30 minutes | Cook time: 1 hour 30 minutes | Serves 4 |
| --- | --- | --- |

- 4 pork chops
- 4 cloves garlic, smashed
- 2 tablespoons olive oil
- ⅓ cup lime juice
- ¼ cup water
- 1 teaspoon ground cumin
- Salt and black pepper

1. Preheat your griddle to medium heat. Generously season the pork chops with salt on both sides and cook them until they are lightly browned. 2. In a bowl, combine water, minced garlic, and lime juice, then whisk together until well mixed. 3. While the pork chops continue to cook, baste them regularly with the lime juice mixture for added flavor. 4. Once the pork chops are fully cooked, remove them from the griddle and drizzle with additional sauce. Finish with a sprinkle of black pepper before serving.

## Sweet & Savory Bacon Wrapped Dates

| Prep time: 30 minutes | Cook time: 30 minutes | Serves 16 |
| --- | --- | --- |

- 1 pound (454 g) thick-sliced bacon, cut in half
- 1 pound (454 g) pitted dates
- 4 ounces (113 g) gorgonzola cheese
- 32 toothpicks

1. Slice each date lengthwise on one side and gently open them up. Take a small piece of cheese and place it in the center of each date. Close the date halves and wrap a half-slice of bacon around the outside, securing it with a toothpick. Lay a sheet of foil over the griddle grates and arrange the wrapped dates in a single layer on top. Cook until the bacon starts to crisp, then carefully flip each wrap to crisp the other side. 2. Once both sides are crispy, remove the wraps to a platter lined with paper towels to absorb excess grease. Allow them to cool slightly before serving for the perfect bite!

## Cajun-Spiced Griddle Pork Chops

| Prep time: 10 minutes | Cook time: 15 minutes | Serves 4 |
| --- | --- | --- |

- 4 pork chops
- 1 tablespoon paprika
- ½ teaspoon ground cumin
- ½ teaspoon dried sage
- ½ teaspoon salt
- ½ teaspoon black pepper
- ½ teaspoon garlic powder
- ¼ teaspoon cayenne pepper
- 1 tablespoon butter
- 1 tablespoon vegetable oil

1. In a medium bowl, mix together paprika, cumin, sage, salt, pepper, garlic, and cayenne pepper to create a flavorful seasoning blend. 2. Preheat your griddle to medium-high heat, then add butter and oil to the surface. 3. Generously rub the seasoning mixture all over the pork chops to ensure they are well-coated. 4. Place the seasoned pork chops on the griddle and cook for 4 to 5 minutes. Flip the chops and continue cooking for an additional 4 minutes until they are cooked through. 5. Once done, remove the pork chops from the griddle and let them rest for 5 minutes before serving to allow the juices to redistribute.

# Basic Juicy NY Strip Steak

Prep time: 45 minutes | Cook time: 8 minutes | Serves 1

- 8 ounces (227 g) NY strip steak
- Olive oil - Sea salt
- Fresh ground black pepper

1. Take the steak out of the refrigerator and allow it to come to room temperature for about 30 to 45 minutes. 2. Preheat the griddle to medium-high heat and brush the surface with olive oil to prevent sticking. 3. Generously season the steak on all sides with salt and freshly cracked pepper for added flavor. 4. Place the steak on the griddle and cook for approximately 4 to 5 minutes without moving it. 5. Flip the steak and cook for another 4 minutes or until it reaches an internal temperature of 125°F to 130°F for medium rare. 6. Once cooked, transfer the steak to a plate and allow it to rest for 5 minutes before slicing and serving.

# Classic Griddle Chopped Cheese Sandwich

Prep time: 15 minutes | Cook time:10 minutes | Serves 3

- 1 pound (454g) ground beef
- 1 small onion, minced
- 1 tablespoon onion powder
- 1 tablespoon garlic powder
- 1 tablespoon pepper
- 1 teaspoon salt
- 9 slices American cheese
- 3 hero rolls, or other similar bread
- butter or cooking oil, as needed
- Toppings
- lettuce
- tomato
- ketchup
- mayonnaise
- pickles
- mushrooms
- bell peppers
- jalapenos
- marinara sauce
- Thousand Island dressing
- breaded mozzarella sticks

1. Preheat the griddle to medium heat and coat the surface with butter or your preferred cooking oil. Place the meat on one side of the griddle while adding the chopped onions to another section. Allow the onions to sauté until they become translucent and fragrant. 2. As the meat cooks, use a spatula or scraper to chop it into small pieces. Season the meat with onion powder, garlic powder, pepper, and salt, continuing to chop and cook until it changes from red to pink and finally to brown. 3. Once the meat is cooked through but still slightly pink, combine it with the sautéed onions. Divide the mixture into three equal portions and top each portion with three slices of cheese, spreading it evenly. Cover the griddle to help the cheese melt more quickly. 4. After the cheese has melted, scoop up one of the meat portions and place it on a slice of bread. Enhance your sandwich by adding any combination of suggested toppings for extra flavor and texture. Enjoy your delicious creation!

# Buttermilk Pork Sirloin Roast

Prep time: 20 minutes | Cook time: 3 hours | Serves 4-6

- 1 (3 to 3½-pounds / 1.36 kg to 1.6 kg) pork sirloin roast

1. Start by trimming all excess fat and silver skin from the pork roast to ensure even cooking. 2. Place the trimmed roast into a 1-gallon sealable plastic bag or a brining container, then add the buttermilk brine. 3. Refrigerate the roast for an extended period, ideally overnight, turning it occasionally to ensure it brines evenly. 4. After brining, remove the pork roast from the brine and gently pat it dry with a paper towel to remove excess moisture. 5. Insert a meat probe into the thickest part of the roast to monitor the internal temperature. 6. Set up the griddle for indirect cooking and preheat it to 225°F. 7. Place the roast on the griddle and smoke it until the internal temperature reaches 145°F, which should take about 3 to 3½ hours. 8. Once cooked, remove the roast and let it rest under a loose foil tent for 15 minutes before slicing against the grain for maximum tenderness. Enjoy your perfectly smoked pork roast!

# Citrus-Marinated Carne Asada

Prep time: 1-2 hours | Cook time: 15 minutes | Serves 4

- 1 pound (454 g) hanger steak or shirt steak
- ¼ cup olive oil
- 1 lime, juiced
- 1 orange, juiced
- 1 garlic clove, finely
- chopped
- ½ teaspoon cumin
- ¼ teaspoon salt
- ¼ teaspoon ground pepper
- handful of fresh cilantro, chopped

1. In a large sealable plastic bag, combine all of the ingredients and seal the bag tightly. Marinate in the refrigerator for 1 to 2 hours to enhance the flavors. 2. Preheat the griddle to medium-high heat. Cook the marinated meat for 3 minutes on each side, or until it is just cooked through. 3. Once cooked, transfer the meat to a cutting board and let it rest for 10 minutes to allow the juices to redistribute. 4. After resting, slice the meat against the grain for maximum tenderness and serve.

# Sticky-Sweet Pork Shoulder

**Prep time: 8 minutes | Cook time: 8 minutes | Serves 6-8**

- 1 (5 pounds / 2.3 kg) Boston Butt pork shoulder

For the marinade:

- 2 tablespoons garlic, minced
- 1 large piece ginger, peeled and chopped
- 1 cup hoisin sauce
- ¾ cup fish sauce
- ⅔ cup honey
- ⅔ cup Shaoxing
- ½ cup chili oil
- ⅓ cup oyster sauce
- ⅓ cup sesame oil

For the glaze:

- ¾ cup dark brown sugar
- 1 tablespoon light molasses

1. Place the pork shoulder, fat side down, on a cutting board with one of the short ends facing you. Using a long, sharp knife, make a shallow cut along the entire length of one long side of the shoulder, keeping the knife about 1" to 1½" above the cutting board. 2. Continue cutting deeper into the meat while lifting and unfurling it with your free hand until the pork shoulder lies flat. 3. In a blender, purée the marinade ingredients and reserve 1½ cups for later use as a glaze; cover and refrigerate this portion. 4. Pour the remaining marinade into a large sealable plastic bag. 5. Add the pork shoulder to the bag, seal it, and marinate in the refrigerator for 8 hours. 6. Preheat the griddle to medium heat; the thermometer should register around 350°F with the cover closed. Remove the pork from the marinade, allowing any excess to drip off. 7. Combine the glaze ingredients with the reserved marinade, stirring until the sugar is dissolved. 8. Place the pork on the griddle and cook for 8 minutes, basting and turning it with tongs every minute or so, until it is thickly coated with the glaze, lightly charred in spots, and warmed through; an instant-read thermometer inserted into the thickest part should read 145°F. 9. Once cooked, transfer the pork to a cutting board and slice it against the grain into ¼-inch thick pieces for serving.

# Herb-Infused Pork Chops with Apple Compote

**Prep time: 5 minutes | Cook time: 20 minutes | Serves 4**

- 4, bone-in pork chops
- 2 honeycrisp apples, peeled, cored and chopped
- ⅓ cup orange juice
- 1 teaspoon chopped fresh
- rosemary
- 1 teaspoon chopped fresh sage
- Sea salt
- Black pepper

1. In a medium saucepan, combine diced apples, fresh herbs, and a splash of orange juice. Cook over medium heat, stirring occasionally, until the apples become soft and the liquid reduces to a light syrup, which should take approximately 10 to 12 minutes. 2. Season the pork chops generously with salt and freshly cracked black pepper to enhance their flavor. 3. Place the seasoned pork chops onto the preheated griddle, cooking them undisturbed until they easily release from the surface, roughly 4 minutes. 4. Carefully flip the chops and continue cooking on the other side for an additional 3 minutes, ensuring they're nicely browned. 5. Once cooked, remove the pork chops and transfer them to a cutting board, covering them loosely with foil to keep warm. 6. Serve the chops topped with the warm apple compote for a delightful contrast of flavors and enjoy!

# Mexican Steak Salad

**Prep time: 10 minutes | Cook time: 10 minutes | Serves 2**

Steak marinade:

- 2 tablespoons olive oil
- 3 garlic cloves, minced
- 2 teaspoons chili powder
- 1 teaspoon ground cumin
- 1 teaspoon kosher salt
- 1 teaspoon freshly ground pepper
- 1½ pounds (680 g) skirt or flap steak, cut into 4-inch lengths
- ½ cup lager beer

Salad:

- 12 ounces (340 g) romaine hearts, trimmed and chopped
- 1 can black beans, drained and rinsed
- 1 pint cherry tomatoes, halved
- 1 large ripe avocado, pitted, peeled, and cut into chunks
- About ⅓ cup crumbled queso fresco
- Chopped fresh cilantro, for garnish
- Kosher salt

Dressing:

- ½ cup plain whole milk yogurt
- ⅓ cup chopped fresh
- cilantro
- Zest of 1 lime
- Juice of 2 limes

1. Begin by preparing the marinade for the steak. Once mixed, allow the steak to marinate for 4 hours or preferably overnight for enhanced flavor. 2. In a large bowl, combine all the salad ingredients and toss them together. Add your favorite dressing and mix well. Portion the salad onto individual plates. Preheat the griddle to high heat. 3. Once hot, place the marinated steak on the griddle and reduce the heat to medium. Cover the steak with foil and cook for 5 minutes. 4. Flip the steak, cover it again with foil, and continue cooking for another 5 minutes until cooked to your desired doneness. 5. After cooking, remove the steak from the griddle and slice it into 2-inch strips. 6. Arrange the steak strips on top of the individual salads, and finish by sprinkling with flaky salt and a dash of black pepper. Garnish with fresh cilantro for an extra pop of flavor.

# Moroccan-Spiced Pork with Harissa Yogurt Sauce

**Prep time: 40 minutes | Cook time: 20 minutes | Serves 6**

- 2 (1 pound / 454 g) pork tenderloins
- 1 teaspoon ground cinnamon
- 1 teaspoon ground cilantro

For Creamy Harissa Sauce:
- 1 cup Greek yogurt (8 ounces / 227 g)
- 1 tablespoon fresh lemon juice
- 1 tablespoon extra-virgin

- 1 teaspoon ground cumin
- 1 teaspoon paprika
- 1 teaspoon sea salt
- 2 tablespoons olive oil

    olive oil
- 1 teaspoon harissa sauce
- 1 clove garlic, minced
- Kosher salt and cracked black pepper

1. In a small mixing bowl, combine all the ingredients for the harissa and set aside to let the flavors meld. 2. In another bowl, mix together the cinnamon, coriander, cumin, paprika, salt, and olive oil until well combined. 3. Rub this spice mixture evenly over the pork tenderloins, then cover and refrigerate for 30 minutes to allow the flavors to penetrate. 4. Preheat the griddle to high heat and place the tenderloins on it, cooking until they are nicely browned, which should take about 8 to 10 minutes. 5. After browning, turn the tenderloins over and cook for an additional 8 to 10 minutes, ensuring they are cooked through. Once done, transfer the tenderloins to a cutting board, cover them loosely with foil, and let them rest for 10 minutes. 6. After resting, slice the tenderloins and serve them with the creamy harissa sauce for a flavorful dish. Enjoy!

# Florentine Ribeye Pork Loin

**Prep time: 30 minutes | Cook time: 1 hour | Serves 6**

- 1 (3 pounds / 1.36 kg) boneless ribeye pork loin roast
- 4 tablespoons extra-virgin olive oil, divided
- 2 tablespoons Pork Dry Rub or your favorite pork seasoning

- 4 bacon slices
- 6 cups fresh spinach
- 1 small red onion, diced
- 6 cloves garlic, cut into thin slivers
- ¾ cup shredded mozzarella cheese

1. Begin by trimming away any excess fat and silver skin from the pork loin for a cleaner cut. 2. Butterfly the pork loin by cutting it open lengthwise, or ask your butcher to do it for you. There are many excellent videos available online that provide detailed instructions on how to butterfly a loin roast. 3. Rub 2 tablespoons of olive oil on both sides of the butterflied roast, then generously season both sides with your chosen rub. 4. In a large griddle, cook the bacon over medium heat until crispy. Once cooked, crumble the bacon and set it aside, reserving the bacon fat for later use. 5. Place the seasoned pork loin on the griddle and cook for 60 to 75 minutes, or until the internal temperature in the thickest part reaches 140°F. 6. After cooking, allow the pork loin to rest under a loose foil tent for 15 minutes before slicing against the grain for optimal tenderness. Enjoy your deliciously prepared pork loin!

# Dijon Beef Burger Patties

**Prep time: 10 minutes | Cook time: 10 minutes | Serves 4**

- 1 pound (454 g) ground beef
- ½ teaspoon pepper
- ¾ tablespoon Worcestershire sauce
- 1 tablespoon Dijon mustard

- ⅛ teaspoon cayenne
- ⅛ teaspoon chili flakes
- 1 tablespoon parsley, chopped
- ½ teaspoon kosher salt

1. In a mixing bowl, combine all the ingredients and stir until they are well blended. 2. Preheat the griddle to high heat to ensure it's ready for cooking. 3. Lightly spray the griddle surface with cooking spray to prevent sticking. 4. Form the mixture into patties and place them on the hot griddle. Cook for 5 minutes on each side until they are golden brown and cooked through. 5. Once done, serve the patties hot and enjoy your delicious meal!

# Griddled Roast Beef Melt

**Prep time: 10 minutes | Cook time: 5 minutes | Serves 1**

- 2 bread slices
- 2 cheese slices
- 4 deli roast beef, sliced

- 2 teaspoons butter
- 1 tablespoon mayonnaise
- ¼ cup caramelized onions, sliced

1. Begin by spreading butter evenly on one side of each slice of bread for added flavor. 2. Take one slice of bread and spread a layer of mayonnaise on the unbuttered side. Top it with slices of beef, onions, and cheese. 3. Place the second slice of bread on top, with the buttered side facing out, to form a sandwich. 4. Preheat the griddle to high heat to ensure it's hot enough for cooking. 5. Lightly spray the griddle surface with cooking spray to prevent sticking. 6. Place the sandwich on the hot griddle and cook for about 5 minutes, or until both sides are golden brown and crispy. 7. Once done, remove the sandwich from the griddle, slice if desired, and serve hot. Enjoy your delicious creation!

# Juicy Beef Burger Pattie

**Prep time: 10 minutes | Cook time: 12 minutes | Serves 6**

- 2 pounds ( 0.9 kg) ground beef
- 2 tablespoons Worcestershire sauce
- ¾ cup onion, chopped
- ½ teaspoon pepper
- ½ teaspoon salt

1. In a mixing bowl, combine all the ingredients and mix thoroughly until everything is well incorporated. 2. Preheat the griddle to high heat to prepare for cooking. 3. Lightly spray the griddle surface with cooking spray to prevent the patties from sticking. 4. Form the mixture into patties and carefully place them on the hot griddle. Cook each patty for 5 minutes on one side, then flip and cook for an additional 5 minutes on the other side until they are golden brown and fully cooked. 5. Once cooked, remove the patties from the griddle and serve hot. Enjoy your delicious meal!

# Ultimate Bacon Beast Burgers

**Prep time: 10 minutes | Cook time:20 minutes | Serves 2**

- 2 large sesame-seed burger buns
- 6 strips bacon
- 1 tablespoon salt
- 1 tablespoon pepper
- 1 tablespoon onion powder
- 1 tablespoon garlic powder
- 2 (⅓-pound / 150g) burger patties
- 4 slices cheese (optional)
- butter, as needed
- Toppings
- mayonnaise
- mustard
- ketchup
- lettuce
- 1 medium, firm tomato, cut into thick slices
- 1 medium, sweet onion, cut into rings
- dill pickle chips

1. Preheat the griddle to medium-high heat and add a generous amount of butter to coat the grilling surface. Place the sesame seed buns on the griddle and cook for 2 to 3 minutes, or until they are golden brown and warmed through. Set the toasted buns aside. 2. Next, add the bacon to the griddle and cook for 6 to 8 minutes, or until it reaches your desired level of crispiness. Once done, set the bacon aside and keep it warm. 3. In a small bowl, mix together salt, pepper, onion powder, and garlic powder. Season both sides of the burger patties with this seasoning blend. Place the patties on the griddle in the area where the bacon was cooked, then cover to retain heat. Cook for 4 to 5 minutes, or until the tops of the burgers start to sweat red juices. 4. Flip the patties, add cheese if desired, and cover again, cooking for an additional 2 to 3 minutes until they reach your preferred doneness. For reference, I typically cook

them to 135°F and check with an instant-read thermometer. 5. To assemble the burger, spread mayo on the bottom half of the bun. Place the cooked burger patty with melted cheese on top, followed by the crispy bacon and any additional toppings of your choice. Finally, cover with the top bun and enjoy your delicious creation!

# Coffee Crusted Skirt Steak

**Prep time: 10 minutes | Cook time: 20 minutes | Serves 8**

- ¼ cup coffee beans, finely ground
- ¼ cup dark brown sugar, firmly packed - ½ teaspoon sea salt
- ⅛ teaspoon ground
- cinnamon
- Pinch cayenne pepper
- ½ pound (227 g) skirt steak, cut into 4 pieces
- 1 tablespoon olive oil

1. Preheat the griddle to high heat. 2. In a bowl, combine coffee, brown sugar, salt, cinnamon, and cayenne pepper to create a flavorful rub. 3. Take the steak out of the refrigerator and let it sit at room temperature for about 15 minutes. Rub the steak with oil, then generously sprinkle the spice rub over it. Massage the rub into the meat for even coverage. 4. Sear the steak on the griddle until it is nicely charred and cooked to medium-rare, approximately 2 to 4 minutes per side. 5. Once cooked, transfer the steak to a cutting board, cover it with foil, and let it rest for 5 minutes. Finally, thinly slice the steak against the grain for the best texture. Enjoy your deliciously seasoned steak!

# Double-Smoked Ham

**Prep time: 15 minutes | Cook time: 2 hours 30 minutes | Serves 8-12**

- 1 (10 pounds / 4.5 kg) smoked, boneless, wholly cooked, ready-to-eat ham or bone-in smoked ham

1. Begin by removing the ham from its packaging and allowing it to sit at room temperature for 30 minutes to ensure even cooking. 2. Set up the griddle for indirect cooking and preheat it to 180°F. 3. Once heated, place the ham directly on the griddle grates and smoke it at this low temperature for 1 hour. 4. After 60 minutes, increase the griddle temperature to 350°F to finish cooking. 5. Continue cooking the ham until it reaches an internal temperature of 140°F, which should take an additional 1½ to 2 hours. 6. Once cooked, remove the ham from the griddle and wrap it in foil. Let it rest for 15 minutes before slicing against the grain for optimal tenderness. Enjoy your delicious smoked ham!

# Tropical Pineapple Beef Burgers

Prep time: 10 minutes | Cook time: 8 minutes | Serves 4

- 1¼ pounds (567 g) ground beef
- 2 pineapple slices, chopped
- ¼ teaspoon pepper
- 1 garlic clove, minced
- 1 teaspoon ginger, grated
- ¼ cup green onions, chopped
- ¼ cup soy sauce
- Salt

1. In a large mixing bowl, combine all the ingredients and mix thoroughly until the mixture is well combined. 2. Preheat the griddle to high heat so it's ready for cooking. 3. Lightly spray the surface of the griddle with cooking spray to prevent sticking. 4. Form the mixture into patties and carefully place them on the hot griddle. Cook each patty for 4 minutes on one side, then flip and cook for an additional 4 minutes on the other side until they are golden and fully cooked. 5. Once cooked, serve the patties hot and enjoy your tasty meal!

# Herb-Crusted Mediterranean Pork Tenderloin

Prep time: 2 hours | Cook time: 30 minutes | Serves 4

- 1 pound (454 g) pork tenderloin
- 1 tablespoon olive oil
- 2 teaspoons dried oregano
- ¾ teaspoon lemon pepper
- 1 teaspoon garlic powder
- ¼ cup parmesan cheese, grated
- 3 tablespoons olive tapenade

1. Lay the pork tenderloin on a large piece of plastic wrap. 2. Drizzle the tenderloin with oil, then evenly sprinkle oregano, garlic powder, and lemon pepper over the entire surface. 3. Wrap the tenderloin tightly in the plastic wrap and refrigerate for 2 hours to allow the flavors to meld. 4. Preheat the griddle to medium-high heat. 5. Once chilled, transfer the pork to a cutting board, remove the plastic wrap, and make a lengthwise cut through the center of the tenderloin, opening it like a book without cutting all the way through. 6. In a small mixing bowl, combine tapenade and Parmesan cheese, then rub this mixture into the center of the tenderloin before folding the meat back together. 7. Secure the tenderloin with kitchen twine, tying it at 2-inch intervals. 8. Sear the tenderloin on the griddle for about 20 minutes, turning it once during cooking, until the internal temperature reaches 145°F. 9. After searing, transfer the tenderloin to a cutting board. 10. Tent the meat with aluminum foil and let it rest for 10 minutes to allow the juices to redistribute. 11. Carefully remove the twine and slice the tenderloin into ¼-inch-thick pieces for serving.

# Herb-Crusted Pork Chops with Apple Compote

Prep time: 5 minutes | Cook time: 20 minutes | Serves 4

- 4 bone-in pork chops
- 2 honeycrisp apples, peeled, cored and chopped
- ⅓ cup orange juice
- 1 teaspoon chopped fresh
- rosemary
- 1 teaspoon chopped fresh sage
- Sea salt
- Black pepper

1. In a saucepan, combine the apples, herbs, and orange juice. Simmer over medium heat until the apples become tender and the juices thicken into a thin syrup, which should take about 10 to 12 minutes. 2. While the apples are cooking, season the pork chops generously with salt and pepper. 3. Place the seasoned pork chops on the preheated griddle and cook until they release easily from the surface, approximately 4 minutes. 4. Flip the chops and continue cooking on the other side for an additional 3 minutes. 5. Once cooked, transfer the pork chops to a cutting board and cover them loosely with foil to keep warm. 6. Serve the pork chops topped with the apple compote for a delicious finish!

# Bacon-Wrapped Jalapeño Smokie Bombs

Prep time: 10 minutes | Cook time: 15 minutes | Serves 10

- 10 fresh jalapenos
- 20 Cheddar Little Smokies
- 8 ounces (227 g) Cream Cheese
- 2 pounds ( 0.9 kg) Bacon (½ strip each)
- ⅛ Sweet Onion (diced)
- 1 tablespoon Sugar

1. Begin by softening the cream cheese, then blend in the sugar and chopped onions until smooth and well combined. 2. Slice the jalapeños in half lengthwise, removing all seeds and membranes, then rinse them under cold water. 3. Spoon 1 teaspoon of the cream cheese mixture into each jalapeño half, then place one smokie on top of the cream cheese and gently press it down. 4. Arrange the prepared jalapeño bombs in a single layer on the griddle. Cook until the bacon starts to crisp up, moving them to a cooler side of the griddle if they begin to flare up. Once done, remove them to a platter lined with paper towels to absorb excess grease. 5. Allow the bombs to cool slightly before serving for a delicious, savory treat!

# Griddled Roast Beef & Tomato Melt

**Prep time: 10 minutes | Cook time: 10 minutes | Serves 2**

- 4 bread slices
- ½ pound (227 g) deli roast beef slices
- 2 tablespoons mayonnaise
- 1 tablespoon butter
- ½ onion, sliced
- 1 tomato, sliced
- 4 cheese slices

1. Begin by spreading butter evenly on one side of each slice of bread for added flavor. 2. Take 4 of the bread slices and spread a layer of mayonnaise on the unbuttered side. Top each with slices of beef, cheese, tomatoes, and onions for a delicious filling. 3. Place the remaining bread slices on top, buttered side facing out, to form sandwiches. 4. Preheat the griddle to high heat to prepare for cooking. 5. Lightly spray the griddle surface with cooking spray to prevent sticking. 6. Carefully place the sandwiches on the hot griddle and cook for about 5 minutes, or until both sides are golden brown and crispy. 7. Once done, remove the sandwiches from the griddle, slice if desired, and serve hot. Enjoy your tasty creation!

# Diner-Style Patty Melt

**Prep time: 8 minutes | Cook time:18 minutes | Serves 2**

- 2 cups sliced mushrooms
- 1 cup sliced sweet onions
- 2 (¼-pound / 113g) ground beef burger patties
- butter, as needed
- 4 slices deli rye or dark rye bread
- 4 slices Swiss cheese
- cooking oil, as needed
- salt and pepper, to taste

1. Preheat the griddle to medium-high heat. 2. Lightly coat the cooking surface with oil, then add the sliced onions and mushrooms, keeping them separate on the griddle. Sprinkle salt and pepper over the mushrooms and onion slices. Sauté the mushrooms for 6 to 8 minutes, stirring and flipping frequently. The salt will draw out moisture from the mushrooms, causing them to shrink and take on a lightly browned color. Cook the onions until they become translucent and slightly caramelized, about 5 minutes. Once done, move the cooked mushrooms and onions to a cooler side of the griddle to keep warm. 3. Season the burger patties with salt and pepper on both sides. Cook them on the griddle for 4 to 6 minutes per side, or until they reach your desired doneness. Once cooked, set them aside to keep warm. 4. To assemble the patty melts, generously butter the griddle and place all four slices of bread on the buttered surface. Top each slice of bread with a slice of Swiss cheese. Divide the sautéed onion and mushroom mixture between two slices of bread, then place a cooked burger patty on top of each of those slices. Finish by placing the remaining slices of bread on top. If you prefer a crispier bread and fully melted cheese, carefully flip the assembled patty melts and allow them to cook for a few more minutes. Covering them during this final cooking stage will help the cheese melt faster. Enjoy your delicious patty melts!

# Mediterranean Flank Steak Gyros

**Prep time: 5 minutes | Cook time: 20 minutes | Serves 4**

- 1 pound (454 g) flank steak
- 1 white onion, thinly sliced
- 1 roma tomato, thinly sliced
- 1 cucumber, peeled and thinly sliced
- ¼ cup crumbled feta cheese
- 6-inch pita pockets

For the marinade:
- ¼ cup olive oil, plus more for brushing
- 1 teaspoon dried oregano
- 1 teaspoon balsamic vinegar
- 1 teaspoon garlic powder
- Sea salt and freshly ground pepper, to taste

For the sauce:
- 1 cup plain yogurt
- 2 tablespoons fresh dill (can use dried), chopped
- 1 teaspoon garlic, minced
- 2 tablespoons lemon juice

1. Begin by slicing the flank steak into thin strips against the grain for maximum tenderness. In a large sealable plastic bag, combine all the marinade ingredients, then add the sliced meat. Seal the bag and turn it to ensure the steak is evenly coated. 2. Refrigerate the marinated steak for 2 hours or overnight to enhance the flavor. 3. Preheat the griddle to medium-high heat, and set your oven to 250°F to warm the pitas. 4. In a small mixing bowl, combine the sauce ingredients and set the mixture aside for later use. 5. Lightly spritz the pitas with water, wrap them in foil, and place them in the oven to warm. 6. Brush the griddle surface with olive oil to prevent sticking. 7. Add the marinated meat to the griddle, discarding any leftover marinade. Cook the steak until it is browned and cooked through, which should take about 5 minutes. 8. Once the pitas are warmed, remove them from the oven and cut them in half. 9. Arrange the pitas on plates, stuffing each with cucumber, tomato, onions, and the cooked beef. Spoon the yogurt sauce over the meat and sprinkle with feta cheese before serving for a delicious and satisfying meal!

# Smashed Burgers

- 4 burger buns
- 1 pound (454g) ground chuck (80/20), divided into
- 4-ounce (113g) balls
- 4 slices American cheese
- salt and pepper, to taste

1. Preheat the griddle to high heat and cut 4 squares of parchment paper. Lightly butter the griddle surface, then toast the insides of the burger buns for 1 to 2 minutes until they develop a golden brown crust and are warmed through. Set the toasted buns aside. 2. Clean the griddle surface using a scraper or spatula. Place ground beef balls on the griddle, spacing them about 6 to 8 inches apart. Lay a square of parchment paper on top of one beef ball and smash it down to about ¼ inch thick using a bacon press. Remove the parchment and repeat with the remaining beef balls. Season the exposed sides of the burgers generously with salt and pepper. 3. Allow the smashed beef patties to cook undisturbed for about 2 minutes. Use a heavy-duty spatula to scrape underneath each burger to release it from the griddle, ensuring to lift all the browned bits along with it. Flip the burgers and quickly repeat this step with the others. 4. Place cheese slices on top of the burgers and continue cooking for another 2 minutes, or until the cheese starts to melt. If you want the cheese extra melty, cover the burgers after adding the cheese. 5. With your heavy-duty spatula, scrape each burger at a steep angle to release them from the griddle, then slide them onto the toasted burger buns. 6. You can add toppings like lettuce, tomato, onion, and various condiments or sauces, but I prefer to savor the rich, meaty flavor of the burger paired with the smooth mouthfeel of the buttery toasted bun.

# Citrus-Marinated Yucatan Griddle Pork

ngredients:
- 2 pork tenderloins, trimmed
- 1 teaspoon annatto powder

For the marinade:
- 2 oranges, juiced
- 2 lemons, juiced, or more to taste
- 2 limes, juiced, or more to taste
- Olive oil
- 6 cloves garlic, minced
- 1 teaspoon ground cumin
- ½ teaspoon cayenne pepper
- ½ teaspoon dried oregano
- ½ teaspoon black pepper

1. In a mixing bowl, combine the marinade ingredients and whisk them together until well blended. 2. Cut the pork tenderloins in half crosswise, then slice each piece in half lengthwise to create smaller portions. 3. Place the pork pieces in the marinade, ensuring they are thoroughly coated with the mixture. 4. Cover the bowl with plastic wrap and refrigerate for 4 to 6 hours to allow the flavors to penetrate. 5. After marinating, transfer the pork pieces to a paper-towel-lined bowl to absorb excess moisture. 6. Discard the paper towels, then drizzle the pork with olive oil and sprinkle a bit more annatto powder on top. 7. Preheat the griddle to medium-high heat and lightly oil the surface. 8. Place the pork pieces evenly spaced on the griddle and cook for 4 to 5 minutes without moving them. 9. Flip the pork and cook on the other side for an additional 4 to 5 minutes until cooked through. 10. Once done, transfer the pork onto a serving platter and allow it to rest for about 5 minutes before serving.

# Ground Pork Banh Mi

- ¼ cup rice wine vinegar
- 3 tablespoons sugar
- 1 cup carrot matchsticks
- ¼ cup mayonnaise
- ½ cup minced cilantro, divided
- 1 tablespoon sriracha
- 1 pound (454g) ground pork shoulder
- ¼ cup grated onion
- 1 clove garlic, minced
- 3 tablespoons soy sauce
- 2 tablespoons fish sauce
- 1 teaspoon salt, divided
- 1 teaspoon pepper
- 4 French bread–style sandwich buns
- cilantro sprigs, for garnish

1. In a microwave-safe container, heat the rice wine vinegar with the sugar and ½ teaspoon of salt until dissolved, which should take about 45 seconds. Pour this warm vinegar mixture over the carrot matchsticks in a medium bowl, then refrigerate to cool the carrots. Meanwhile, in a small bowl, combine mayonnaise with 1 tablespoon of minced cilantro and sriracha; mix well and set aside in the refrigerator. 2. In a large mixing bowl, combine the ground pork with the remaining minced cilantro, onion, garlic, soy sauce, fish sauce, the remaining salt, and pepper. Cover the mixture and let it rest in the refrigerator for 1 hour or overnight to allow the flavors to develop. 3. Preheat the griddle to medium-high heat. Using a spatula, chop and sauté the pork mixture for about 5 minutes, then cover the pan and continue cooking for an additional 4 to 6 minutes, adding a splash of water to the griddle to help steam the meat. 4. While the pork is cooking, cut the sandwich buns in half and warm them on the griddle until heated through and lightly colored. Spread the cilantro mayonnaise on one side of each bun, then top with ¼ of the pork mixture on each. Finish by garnishing with the pickled carrots and fresh cilantro sprigs for a delicious and vibrant sandwich!

# Rosemary Garlic Marinated Flank Steak

- 2 (8 ounces / 227 g) flank steaks
- For the marinade:
- 1 tablespoon extra virgin olive oil, plus more for brushing
- 2 tablespoons fresh rosemary, chopped
- 2 cloves garlic, minced
- 2 teaspoons sea salt
- ¼ teaspoon black pepper

1. In a food processor or blender, combine the marinade ingredients and pulse until the garlic and rosemary are finely pulverized. 2. Use a fork to pierce each steak 10 times on both sides to allow the marinade to penetrate. 3. Rub the marinade evenly over each steak, coating both sides thoroughly. 4. Place the marinated steaks in a covered dish and refrigerate for at least 1 hour, or preferably overnight for deeper flavor. 5. Preheat the griddle to high heat, then brush it with olive oil to prevent sticking. 6. Cook the steaks on the griddle for 5 minutes, then flip them over, tent with foil, and cook for an additional 3 to 4 minutes for the desired doneness. 7. Once cooked, transfer the steaks to a cutting board and cover with aluminum foil. Let them rest for about 15 minutes to allow the juices to redistribute. 8. After resting, slice the steaks very thinly against the grain and serve immediately for maximum tenderness.

# Peach-Glazed Mojo Pork Shoulder

- 1 (6 pounds / 2.7 kg) pork shoulder
- 1 quart Hawaiian Mojo
- ½ cup sea-salt
- 1 can peach slices, in syrup
- 2 tablespoon garlic powder
- 2 tablespoon red pepper flakes
- 15 ounces (425 g) sliced peaches in syrup
- 16 ounces (453 g) peach preserves
- 12 ounces (340 g) apricot & pineapple preserves
- ½ cup Stubbs Mesquite Liquid Smoke

1. Begin by injecting the pork shoulder with mojo marinade, ensuring it's well infused. Marinate the pork overnight for maximum flavor. Just before roasting, allow the pork to come to room temperature. Smoke the pork shoulder for 5 to 6 hours, or until the internal temperature reaches 185°F for optimal tenderness. 2. Once cooked, slice the pork and pile it into a pan. Generously slather the top with peach-pineapple glaze, ensuring an even coating. Place the pan under a hot broiler for 5 to 10 minutes to caramelize and brown the glaze for added flavor. 3. Serve the glazed pork with sweet Hawaiian rolls and fluffy white rice for a delicious meal that everyone will love!

# Pineapple Bacon Pork Chops

- 1 large whole pineapple
- 6 pork chops

For the glaze:
- ¼ cup honey
- 12 slices thick-cut bacon
- Toothpicks, soaked in water
- ⅛ teaspoon cayenne pepper

1. Set both burners to medium-high heat and allow them to preheat for about 15 minutes. After that, turn off one of the middle burners and reduce the remaining burners to medium. 2. Cut off the top and bottom of the pineapple, then peel it by slicing off the skin in strips. 3. Slice the pineapple flesh into six quarters. 4. Wrap each quarter of pineapple with a slice of bacon, securing both ends with a toothpick. 5. Brush the wrapped pineapple with honey and sprinkle cayenne pepper on top for added flavor. 6. Place the pineapple quarters on the griddle, flipping them when the bacon is cooked to ensure both sides are evenly cooked. 7. While the pineapple is grilling, coat the pork chops with honey and sprinkle them with cayenne pepper before placing them on the griddle. 8. Tent the pork chops with foil and cook for 20 minutes. Flip the chops and continue cooking for an additional 10 to 20 minutes, or until they are fully cooked through. 9. Serve each pork chop alongside a bacon-wrapped pineapple quarter for a delicious combination!

# Spicy Habanero-Glazed Pork Chops

Prep time: 30 minutes | Cook time: 13 minutes | Serves 4

- 4½-inch-thick bone-in pork chops
- 3 tablespoons olive oil, plus more for griddle

For the marinade:

- 1 habanero chili, seeded, chopped fine
- 2 garlic cloves, minced
- ½ cup fresh orange juice

- Kosher salt and freshly ground black pepper

- 2 tablespoons brown sugar
- 1 tablespoon apple cider vinegar

1. In a large sealable plastic bag, mix together all the marinade ingredients until well combined. 2. Use a fork to pierce the pork chops all over to allow the marinade to penetrate, then place them in the bag. Seal the bag and turn it to ensure the chops are evenly coated. 3. Allow the pork chops to marinate at room temperature for 30 minutes, turning the bag occasionally to distribute the marinade. 4. Preheat your griddle to medium-high heat to prepare for cooking. 5. Lightly brush the griddle surface with oil to prevent sticking. 6. After marinating, remove the pork chops from the bag and gently pat them dry with paper towels to eliminate excess moisture. 7. Place the chops on the griddle and sear them for 8 minutes, turning occasionally, until they are nicely charred and cooked through. 8. Once done, transfer the pork chops to a plate and let them rest for 5 minutes to allow the juices to redistribute. 9. Serve the pork chops alongside your favorite side dishes for a complete meal!

# Molasses-Glazed Country Ribs

Prep time: 10 minutes | Cook time: 4 hours | Serves 6

- 3 pounds (1.4 kg) country-style pork ribs
- 1 cup low-sugar ketchup
- ½ cup water
- ¼ cup onion, finely chopped
- ¼ cup cider vinegar or wine vinegar

- ¼ cup light molasses
- 2 tablespoons Worcestershire sauce
- 2 teaspoons chili powder
- 2 cloves garlic, minced

1. In a saucepan, combine ketchup, water, onion, vinegar, molasses, Worcestershire sauce, chili powder, and garlic. Bring the mixture to a boil, then reduce the heat and let it simmer uncovered for 10 to 15 minutes, stirring frequently, until it reaches your desired thickness. 2. Trim any excess fat from the ribs to ensure even cooking. 3. Preheat the griddle to medium-high heat to prepare for cooking. 4. Place the ribs on the griddle, bone-side down, and cook for 1½ to 2 hours, or until they become tender. During the last 10 minutes of cooking, brush the ribs with the prepared sauce to enhance their flavor. 5. Once done, serve the ribs with any remaining sauce on the side for dipping and enjoy your delicious meal!

# BBQ Sauce Pork Chops

Prep time: 4 hours | Cook time: 15 minutes | Serves 6

- 6 boneless pork chops, thick
- 1 tablespoon salt and sugar
- Pepper to taste

- 1 cup water
- 1 cup sweet barbecue sauce
- ¼ cup cider vinegar

1. Place the pork chops in a resealable bag with 1 cup of water and the boiled and cooled sugar mixture. Allow the chops to brine for 4 hours to enhance their flavor and tenderness. 2. Preheat your griddle to high heat to ensure it's ready for cooking. 3. In a small saucepan, combine the barbecue sauce and vinegar. Bring the mixture to a simmer and let it cook uncovered for 20 to 30 minutes, stirring frequently to prevent sticking. 4. Before placing the pork chops on the griddle, lightly brush the grates with oil to prevent sticking. 5. Cook the pork chops over high heat for 10 to 12 minutes, turning them once halfway through for even cooking. Just before removing the chops from the griddle, brush them with the prepared sauce for added flavor. 6. Serve the chops with the remaining barbecue sauce on the side for dipping and enjoy your delicious meal!

# Chapter 4

# Fish and Seafood

# Chapter 4 Fish and Seafood

## Spicy Cilantro Yogurt Sauce

| Prep time: 10 minutes | Cook time: 20 minutes | Serves 4 |
| --- |

- Vegetable oil (for the griddle)
- 2 serrano chilis
- 2 garlic cloves
- 1 cup cilantro leaves
- ½ cup plain whole-milk Greek yogurt
- 1 tablespoon of extra virgin
- olive oil
- 1 teaspoon honey
- Kosher salt
- 2 (12 ounces / 340 g) bone-in salmon steaks
- Intolerances:
- Gluten-Free
- Egg-Free

1. Preheat the griddle to medium-high heat and lightly oil the grate to prevent sticking. 2. Remove the seeds from one chili and discard them. In a blender, combine the two chilis, garlic, cilantro, yogurt, oil, honey, and ¼ cup of water. Blend until smooth, then season the mixture with salt to taste. 3. Set aside half of the sauce in a small bowl for later use. Season the salmon steaks with salt to enhance their flavor. 4. Place the salmon steaks on the griddle, cooking for about 4 minutes while turning them occasionally until they begin to turn dark. 5. Continue cooking the salmon, turning frequently and basting with the reserved sauce for at least 4 more minutes, or until fully cooked through. Enjoy your delicious salmon with the vibrant chili sauce!

## Griddled Lobster Tails with Lime Basil Butter

| Prep time: 5 minutes | Cook time: 6 minutes | Serves 4 |
| --- |

- 4 lobster tails (cut in half lengthwise)
- 3 tablespoons olive oil
- Lime wedges (to serve) - Sea salt, to taste
- For the lime basil butter:
- 1 stick unsalted butter,
- softened
- ½ bunch basil, roughly chopped
- 1 lime, zested and juiced
- 2 cloves garlic, minced
- ¼ teaspoon red pepper flakes

1. In a mixing bowl, combine all the ingredients for the butter and mix well; set aside until you're ready to use it. 2. Preheat the griddle to medium-high heat to prepare for cooking the lobster tails. 3. Drizzle the lobster tail halves with olive oil and season generously with salt and pepper to enhance their flavor. 4. Place the lobster tails, flesh-side down, on the hot griddle. 5. Allow them to cook until the flesh becomes opaque, which should take about 3 minutes. Flip the tails over and cook for another 3 minutes to ensure they are cooked through. 6. In the last minute of cooking, add a dollop of the lime basil butter on top of the lobster tails, allowing it to melt into the meat. Serve immediately for a delicious seafood dish!

## Shrimp with Shrimp Butter

| Prep time: 15 minutes | Cook time: 1 5 minutes | Serves 4 |
| --- |

- 6 tablespoon unsalted butter
- ½ cup finely chopped red onion
- 1½ teaspoons crushed red pepper
- 1 teaspoon Malaysian shrimp paste
- 1½ teaspoons lime juice
- salt
- grounded black pepper
- 24 shelled and deveined large shrimp
- 6 wooden skewers(better if soaked in water for 30 minutes)
- Torn mint leaves and assorted sprouts
- Intolerances:
- Gluten-Free - Egg-Free

1. In a small griddle, melt 3 tablespoons of butter over moderate heat. Add the chopped onion and cook for about 3 minutes until it becomes translucent. 2. Stir in the crushed red pepper and shrimp paste, cooking for an additional 2 minutes until fragrant. 3. Add lime juice and the remaining 3 tablespoons of butter, seasoning with salt to taste. Keep the shrimp sauce warm while you prepare the shrimp. 4. Prepare the griddle by preheating it. Season the shrimp with salt and pepper, then thread them onto skewers, making sure not to pack them too tightly. 5. Grill the shrimp over high heat, turning them once, until they are lightly charred and cooked through, which should take about 4 minutes. 6. Once cooked, transfer the shrimp to a platter and generously spoon the shrimp sauce over them. Garnish with fresh mint leaves and sprouts before serving for a refreshing touch. Enjoy!

# Blackened Salmon

**Prep time: 10 minutes | Cook time: 10 minutes | Serves 5**

- 1¼ pounds (567 g) salmon fillets
- 2 tablespoons blackened
- seasoning
- 2 tablespoons butter

1. Generously season the salmon fillets with blackened seasoning to enhance their flavor. 2. Preheat the griddle to high heat to ensure it's ready for cooking. 3. Melt a pat of butter on the griddle surface to prevent sticking and add richness to the fish. 4. Place the seasoned salmon fillets onto the hot griddle and cook for 4 to 5 minutes, allowing a nice crust to form. 5. Carefully turn the salmon fillets and continue cooking for an additional 4 to 5 minutes until they are cooked through and flaky. 6. Once done, remove from the griddle and serve immediately. Enjoy your flavorful blackened salmon!

# Pesto Shrimp

**Prep time: 10 minutes | Cook time: 5 minutes | Serves 4**

- 1 pound (454 g) shrimp, remove shells and tails
- ½ cup basil pesto
- Pepper
- Salt

1. In a large bowl, combine shrimp, pesto, pepper, and salt, tossing well to coat. Set aside to marinate for 15 minutes to enhance the flavors. 2. Preheat the griddle over medium-high heat to get it ready for cooking. 3. Thread the marinated shrimp onto skewers, ensuring they are evenly spaced. Place the skewers on the hot griddle and cook for 1 to 2 minutes on each side, or until the shrimp are pink and cooked through. 4. Once done, remove from the griddle and serve immediately. Enjoy your delicious shrimp skewers!

# Spicy Lemon Butter Shrimp

**Prep time: 10 minutes | Cook time: 10 minutes | Serves 4**

- 1½ pounds (680 g) shrimp, peeled and deveined
- 3 garlic cloves, minced
- 1 small onion, minced
- ½ cup butter
- 1½ tablespoons fresh parsley, chopped
- 1 tablespoon fresh lemon juice
- ¼ teaspoon red pepper flakes
- Pepper
- Salt

1. Preheat the griddle to high heat to get it ready for cooking. 2. Melt a generous amount of butter on the griddle surface. 3. Add minced garlic, diced onion, red chili flakes, pepper, and salt to the melted butter, stirring for about 2 minutes until fragrant. 4. Season the shrimp with additional salt and pepper, then thread them onto skewers. 5. Brush the shrimp skewers with the flavorful butter mixture to enhance their taste. 6. Place the shrimp skewers on the hot griddle and cook until the shrimp turns pink and opaque, approximately 3 to 4 minutes. 7. Once cooked, transfer the shrimp to a serving plate. 8. Drizzle fresh lemon juice over the shrimp and garnish with chopped parsley for a fresh finish. 9. Serve immediately and enjoy your delicious shrimp skewers!

# Zesty Lemon Garlic Scallops

**Prep time: 10 minutes | Cook time: 5 minutes | Serves 2**

- 1 pound (454 g) frozen bay scallops, thawed, rinsed & pat dry
- 1 teaspoon garlic, minced
- 2 tablespoons olive oil
- 1 teaspoon parsley, chopped
- 1 teaspoon lemon juice
- Pepper
- Salt

1. Preheat the griddle to high heat to prepare for cooking. 2. Add a drizzle of oil to the griddle surface to prevent sticking. 3. Once the oil is hot, add minced garlic and sauté for about 30 seconds until fragrant. 4. Add the scallops to the griddle, along with lemon juice, pepper, and salt. Sauté until the scallops turn opaque and are cooked through, which should take just a few minutes. 5. Remove from the heat, garnish with fresh parsley, and serve immediately for a delicious seafood dish!

# Lemon Garlic Butter Tilapia

**Prep time: 10 minutes | Cook time: 8 minutes | Serves 6**

- 2 pounds ( 0.9 kg) tilapia fillets
- 1 teaspoon garlic powder
- ½ fresh lemon juice
- 1 tablespoon butter, melted
- Pepper - Salt

1. In a small bowl, mix together lemon juice, garlic powder, and melted butter. Microwave for 10 seconds to warm the mixture slightly. 2. Brush both sides of the fish fillet with the lemon mixture, then season with salt and pepper to taste. 3. Preheat the griddle to high heat to ensure it's hot enough for cooking. 4. Lightly spray the griddle surface with cooking spray to prevent sticking. 5. Place the seasoned fish fillets on the hot griddle and cook for 4 minutes on each side, or until the fish is cooked through and flakes easily with a fork. 6. Once cooked, remove from the griddle and serve immediately. Enjoy your flavorful fish dish!

# Buttered Clams

- 24 littleneck clams
- ½ cup cold butter, chopped
- 2 tablespoons fresh parsley, minced
- 3 garlic cloves, minced
- 1 teaspoon fresh lemon juice

1. Preheat the griddle to 450°F to prepare for cooking. 2. Scrub the clams thoroughly under cold running water to remove any sand or debris. 3. In a large casserole dish, mix together the remaining ingredients that you plan to use for flavoring the clams. 4. Place the casserole dish on the griddle to warm it up. 5. Arrange the cleaned clams directly onto the hot griddle and cook for about 5 to 8 minutes, or until the clams open up. Discard any clams that do not open during cooking. 6. Using tongs, carefully transfer the opened clams into the casserole dish, then remove it from the griddle. 7. Serve the clams immediately for the best flavor and freshness. Enjoy!

# Halibut Fillets with Spinach and Olives

- 4 (6 ounces / 170 g) halibut fillets
- ⅓ cup olive oil
- 4 cups baby spinach
- ¼ cup lemon juice
- 2 ounces (57 g) pitted black
- olives, halved
- 2 tablespoons flat leaf parsley, chopped
- 2 teaspoons fresh dill, chopped
- Lemon wedges, to serve

1. Preheat the griddle to medium heat to prepare for cooking. 2. In a mixing bowl, toss the spinach with lemon juice and set it aside to marinate slightly. 3. Brush the fish fillets with olive oil and place them on the griddle. Cook for 3 to 4 minutes on each side, or until the fish is cooked through and flakes easily. 4. Once cooked, remove the fish from the griddle, cover with foil, and let it rest for 5 minutes to retain its moisture. 5. In the same griddle, add the remaining olive oil and cook the spinach for about 2 minutes, or until it is just wilted. Remove from heat. 6. Toss the cooked spinach with olives and fresh herbs for added flavor, then transfer it to serving plates alongside the fish. Serve with lemon wedges for a fresh finish. Enjoy your meal!

# BBQ Butter Shrimp

- 8 ounces (227 g) salted butter, melted
- ¼ cup Worcestershire sauce
- ¼ cup fresh parsley, chopped
- 1 lemon, quartered
- 2 pounds ( 0.9 kg) jumbo shrimp, peeled and deveined
- 3 tablespoons BBQ rub

1. In a metal baking pan, combine all ingredients except for the shrimp and BBQ rub, mixing well to create a flavorful base. 2. Season the shrimp evenly with the BBQ rub to enhance their flavor. 3. Add the seasoned shrimp to the pan with the butter mixture, ensuring each shrimp is well coated. 4. Set the pan aside to marinate for about 20 to 30 minutes, allowing the flavors to meld. 5. Preheat the griddle to 250°F to prepare for cooking. 6. Once heated, place the pan onto the griddle and cook for approximately 25 to 30 minutes, or until the shrimp are cooked through. 7. Carefully remove the pan from the griddle and serve hot for a delicious dish. Enjoy!

# Basil Parmesan Grilled Shrimp

- 1 pound (454 g) shrimp, peeled and deveined
- 2 tablespoons parmesan cheese, grated
- 1 tablespoon fresh lemon juice
- 1 tablespoon pine nuts,
- toasted
- 1 garlic clove
- ½ cup basil
- 1 tablespoon olive oil
- Pepper
- Salt

1. In a blender, combine basil, lemon juice, cheese, pine nuts, garlic, pepper, and salt, then blend until smooth to create a flavorful basil paste. 2. In a mixing bowl, add the shrimp and the prepared basil paste, mixing well to ensure the shrimp are evenly coated. 3. Cover the bowl and place it in the fridge for 20 minutes to allow the flavors to meld. 4. Preheat the griddle to high heat in preparation for cooking. 5. Lightly spray the griddle surface with cooking spray to prevent sticking. 6. Thread the marinated shrimp onto skewers and arrange them on the hot griddle. 7. Cook the shrimp for 3 minutes on each side or until they are fully cooked and opaque. 8. Once done, remove from the griddle and serve immediately. Enjoy your delicious basil shrimp skewers!

# Simple Mahi-Mahi

**Prep time: 10 minutes | Cook time: 10 minutes | Serves 4**

- 4 (6 ounces / 170 g) mahi-mahi fillets
- 2 tablespoons olive oil
- Salt and ground black pepper, as required

1. Preheat the griddle to 350°F to prepare for cooking the fish. 2. Coat the fish fillets evenly with olive oil, then season both sides with salt and black pepper to enhance their flavor. 3. Place the seasoned fish fillets onto the hot griddle and cook for approximately 5 minutes on each side, or until they are golden brown and cooked through. 4. Once done, carefully remove the fish fillets from the griddle and serve them hot for a delicious meal. Enjoy!

# Chili-Infused Grilled Crab Legs

**Prep time: 5 minutes | Cook time: 5 minutes | Serves 4**

- 4 pounds (1.81 kg) king crab legs, cooked
- 2 tablespoons chili oil

1. Preheat the griddle to high heat to ensure it's hot enough for cooking. 2. Brush both sides of the crab legs with chili oil for added flavor, then place them on the griddle. Tent the legs with foil to help retain heat and moisture. 3. Cook the crab legs for 4 to 5 minutes, turning them once halfway through for even cooking. 4. Once cooked, transfer the crab legs to plates and serve with drawn butter for dipping. Enjoy your delicious seafood dish!

# Almond-Crusted Salmon Patties

**Prep time: 10 minutes | Cook time: 10 minutes | Serves 2**

- 6 ounces (170 g) can salmon, drained, remove bones, and pat dry
- 2 tablespoons mayonnaise
- ½ cup almond flour
- ¼ teaspoon thyme
- 1 egg, lightly beaten
- 2 tablespoons olive oil
- Pepper - Salt

1. In a mixing bowl, combine the salmon, thyme, egg, mayonnaise, almond flour, pepper, and salt. Mix well until all ingredients are thoroughly combined. 2. Preheat the griddle to high heat to prepare for cooking. 3. Add a drizzle of oil to the griddle surface to prevent sticking. 4. Form the salmon mixture into small patties and carefully place them onto the hot griddle. Cook for 5 to 6 minutes

until they develop a golden brown crust. 5. Flip the patties and continue cooking for an additional 3 to 4 minutes, until they are cooked through. 6. Once done, remove the patties from the griddle and serve immediately. Enjoy your delicious salmon patties!

# Slow-Cooked Sesame Crusted Flounder

**Prep time: 15 minutes | Cook time: 3 hours | Serves 4**

- ½ cup sesame seeds, toasted
- ½ teaspoon kosher salt flakes
- 1 tablespoon canola oil
- 1 teaspoon sesame oil
- 4 (6 ounces / 170 g) flounder fillets

1. Preheat the griddle to 225°F to prepare for slow cooking. 2. Using a mortar and pestle, lightly crush the sesame seeds with kosher salt to release their flavor. 3. In a small bowl, combine both oils and mix well. 4. Generously coat the fish fillets with the oil mixture, then rub the sesame seed and salt mixture over the fillets for added flavor and texture. 5. Place the seasoned fish fillets onto the lower rack of the griddle and cook for about 2 to 2½ hours, allowing the flavors to meld as the fish cooks slowly. 6. Once cooked, carefully remove the fish fillets from the griddle and serve them hot for a delicious meal. Enjoy!

# Flavorful Mexican Shrimp

**Prep time: 10 minutes | Cook time: 12 minutes | Serves 4**

- 1 pound (454 g) shrimp, cleaned
- 3 tablespoon fresh parsley, chopped
- 1 tablespoon garlic, minced
- ¼ onion, sliced
- ¼ teaspoon paprika
- ¼ teaspoon ground cumin
- 2 fresh lime juice
- 2 tablespoons olive oil
- ¼ cup butter
- Pepper - Salt

1. Season the shrimp with paprika, cumin, pepper, and salt to enhance their flavor. 2. Preheat the griddle to high heat to get it ready for cooking. 3. Add a combination of oil and butter to the hot griddle surface to create a flavorful base. 4. Once the butter is melted, add diced onion and minced garlic, sautéing them for about 5 minutes until the onion is translucent and fragrant. 5. Add the seasoned shrimp to the griddle and cook for 5 to 8 minutes, stirring occasionally, until they turn pink and are fully cooked. 6. Once cooked, add fresh parsley and a squeeze of lime juice to brighten the dish. 7. Stir well to combine all the ingredients, then serve immediately for a delicious shrimp dish! Enjoy!

# Griddled Cod with Onion Butter Sauce

- ¼ cupbutter
- 1 finely chopped small onion
- ¼ cupwhite wine
- 4 (6 ounces) cod fillets

- 1 tablespoonof extra virgin olive oil
- ½ teaspoonsalt (or to taste)
- ½ teaspoonblack pepper
- Lemon wedges

Intolerances:
- Gluten-Free - Egg-Free

1. Preheat the griddle to medium-high heat to get it ready for cooking. 2. In a small griddle, melt the butter and add the diced onion. Cook for 1 to 2 minutes until the onion becomes translucent. 3. Pour in the white wine and let it simmer for an additional 3 minutes. Remove from heat and allow the mixture to cool for about 5 minutes. 4. Drizzle the fish fillets with extra virgin olive oil and season them with salt and pepper. Place the fish on a well-oiled rack on the griddle and cook for 8 minutes. 5. Carefully spoon some of the sauce over the fish and flip it over. Cook for another 6 to 7 minutes, turning occasionally, until the fish reaches an internal temperature of 145°F (63°C). 6. Once cooked, remove the fish from the griddle, top with lemon wedges, and serve immediately for a delicious meal! Enjoy!

# Wine Brined Salmon

- 2 cups low-sodium soy sauce
- 1 cup dry white wine
- 1 cup water
- ½ teaspoon Tabasco sauce
- ⅓ cup sugar

- ¼ cup salt
- ½ teaspoon garlic powder
- ½ teaspoon onion powder
- Ground black pepper, as required
- 4 (6 ounces / 170 g) salmon fillets

1. In a large bowl, combine all ingredients except for the salmon, stirring until the sugar is completely dissolved. 2. Add the salmon fillets to the bowl, ensuring they are well coated with the brine mixture. 3. Cover the bowl and refrigerate the salmon overnight to allow it to absorb the flavors. 4. After brining, remove the salmon from the bowl and rinse it under cold running water to remove excess brine. 5. Pat the salmon fillets dry with paper towels to ensure a nice sear. 6. Set up a wire rack in a sheet pan to allow for proper air circulation. 7. Place the salmon fillets on the wire rack, skin side down, and let them cool for about 1 hour to help develop a pellicle for better smoking. 8. Preheat the griddle to 165°F to prepare for cooking. 9. Once preheated, arrange the salmon fillets on the griddle, skin side down, and cook for about 3 to 5 hours, or until they reach your desired level of doneness. 10. After cooking, carefully remove the salmon fillets from the griddle and serve hot for a delicious meal. Enjoy!

# Griddled Scallops with Lemony Salsa Verde

- 2 tablespoons of vegetable oil and more for the griddle
- 12 large sea scallops, side muscle removed

- Kosher salt and grounded black pepper
- Lemony Salsa Verde

Intolerances:
- Gluten-Free - Egg-Free - Lactose-Free

1. Preheat the griddle to medium-high heat and oil the grate to prevent sticking. On a rimmed baking sheet, toss the scallops with 2 tablespoons of oil and season generously with salt and pepper. 2. Using a fish spatula or your hands, carefully place the seasoned scallops onto the hot griddle. 3. Cook the scallops, occasionally turning them, until they are lightly browned and cooked through, which should take about 2 minutes on each side. 4. Once done, remove the scallops from the griddle and serve them with Lemony Salsa Verde for a fresh and zesty accompaniment. Enjoy your delicious scallops!

# Zesty Lemon Garlic Shrimp

- 1½ pounds (680 g) shrimp, peeled and deveined
- 1 tablespoon garlic, minced
- ¼ cup butter
- ¼ cup fresh parsley,

- chopped
- ¼ cup fresh lemon juice
- Pepper
- Salt

1. Preheat the griddle to high heat to prepare for cooking. 2. Melt a generous amount of butter on the griddle surface. 3. Once the butter is melted, add minced garlic and sauté for about 30 seconds until fragrant. 4. Add the shrimp to the griddle, seasoning them with pepper and salt. Cook for 4 to 5 minutes, or until the shrimp turn pink and opaque. 5. Squeeze in fresh lemon juice and add chopped parsley, stirring well. Cook for an additional 2 minutes to allow the flavors to meld. 6. Remove from the griddle and serve immediately for a delicious shrimp dish. Enjoy!

# Grilled Oregano Shrimp Skewers

Prep time: 10 minutes | Cook time: 7 minutes | Serves 6

- 1½ pounds (680 g) shrimp, peeled and deveined
- 1 tablespoon dried oregano
- 2 teaspoons garlic paste
- 2 lemon juice
- ¼ cup olive oil
- 1 teaspoon paprika
- Pepper
- Salt

1. In a mixing bowl, combine all ingredients thoroughly, then cover and refrigerate for 1 hour to allow the flavors to meld together. 2. After marinating, remove the shrimp from the refrigerator and thread them onto skewers for easy grilling. 3. Preheat the griddle to high heat, preparing it for cooking the shrimp. 4. Once hot, place the skewers on the griddle and cook for 5 to 7 minutes, turning occasionally, until the shrimp are pink and cooked through. 5. After cooking, transfer the skewers to a serving platter. Garnish with fresh herbs or a squeeze of lemon juice for an extra burst of flavor. Enjoy your delicious grilled shrimp skewers!

# Spiced Salmon Kebabs

Prep time: 20 minutes | Cook time: 25 minutes | Serves 4

- 2 tablespoons of chopped fresh oregano
- 2 teaspoons of sesame seeds
- 1 teaspoon ground cumin
- 1 teaspoon Kosher salt
- ¼ teaspoon crushed red pepper flakes
- 1½ pounds (680 g) of skinless salmon fillets, cut into 1" pieces
- 2 lemons, thinly sliced into rounds
- 2 tablespoons of olive oil
- 16 bamboo skewerssoaked in water for one hour

Intolerances:
- Gluten-Free
- Egg-Free
- Lactose-Free

1. Preheat the griddle to medium heat. In a small bowl, mix together oregano, sesame seeds, cumin, salt, and red pepper flakes to create a flavorful spice blend. Set this spice blend aside for later use. 2. Thread the salmon pieces and lemon slices onto 8 sets of parallel skewers to form 8 kebabs, alternating between the salmon and lemon for a burst of flavor. 3. Drizzle the kebabs with oil and generously season them with the prepared spice blend, ensuring an even coating. 4. Place the kebabs on the griddle and cook, turning them occasionally, until the fish is cooked through and flakes easily with a fork. Enjoy your delicious salmon kebabs!

# Greek Salmon Fillets

Prep time: 10 minutes | Cook time: 6 minutes | Serves 2

- 2 salmon fillets
- 1 tablespoon fresh basil, minced
- 1 tablespoon butter, melted
- 1 tablespoon fresh lemon juice
- ⅛ teaspoon salt

1. Preheat the griddle to high heat to ensure it's hot enough for cooking. 2. In a small bowl, combine lemon juice, chopped basil, melted butter, and a pinch of salt, mixing well to create a flavorful marinade. 3. Brush the salmon fillets generously with the lemon mixture, ensuring they are well coated, then place them on the hot griddle. 4. Cook the salmon for 2 to 3 minutes without moving it, then flip the fillets and cook for an additional 2 to 3 minutes, or until the salmon is cooked through and flakes easily with a fork. 5. Once done, remove the salmon from the griddle and serve immediately. Enjoy your delicious, herb-infused salmon!

# Zesty Mexican Shrimp Tacos

Prep time: 10 minutes | Cook time: 10 minutes | Serves 4

- 2 pounds ( 0.9 kg) medium shrimp, peeled and deveined
- 8 flour tortillas, warmed
- 1 bag cabbage slaw
- 1 cup salsa
- 1 cup Mexican crema

For marinade:
- 2 tablespoons olive oil
- 1 tablespoon chili powder
- 1 tablespoon cumin
- 1 tablespoon garlic powder
- 1 tablespoon fresh lime juice
- ¼ teaspoon sea salt
- ⅛ teaspoon fresh ground pepper

1. Preheat a griddle to medium-high heat to prepare for cooking. 2. In a large sealable plastic bag, combine the oil marinade ingredients, then add the shrimp and toss to coat them evenly. Let the shrimp marinate in the refrigerator for 30 minutes to absorb the flavors. 3. Once marinated, cook the shrimp on the hot griddle for about 3 minutes on each side, or until they are fully cooked and opaque. 4. After cooking, transfer the shrimp to a plate and set aside. 5. On each plate, lay out two tortillas. Evenly divide the cooked shrimp, cabbage slaw, and salsa in the center of each tortilla. 6. Drizzle the assembled tacos with Mexican crema for extra flavor, then serve immediately. Enjoy your delicious shrimp tacos!

# Cuttlefish with Spinach and Pine Nuts Salad

Prep time: 15 minutes | Cook time: 30 minutes | Serves 6

- ½ cup of olive oil
- 1 tablespoon of lemon juice
- 1 teaspoon oregano
- Pinch of salt
- 8 large cuttlefish, cleaned
- Spinach, pine nuts, olive oil and vinegar for serving

Intolerances:
- Gluten-Free
- Egg-Free
- Lactose-Free

1. In a bowl, prepare the marinade by combining olive oil, lemon juice, oregano, and a pinch of salt and pepper (keeping in mind that cuttlefish don't require much salt). 2. Add the cuttlefish to the marinade, tossing to ensure they are evenly coated. Cover the bowl and let them marinate for about 1 hour. 3. After marinating, remove the cuttlefish from the marinade and pat them dry using paper towels to remove excess moisture. 4. Preheat the griddle to high heat, closing the lid for 10 to 15 minutes to allow it to reach the desired temperature. 5. Once hot, griddle the cuttlefish for just 3 to 4 minutes on each side, cooking until they are tender and nicely charred. 6. Serve the cooked cuttlefish hot alongside sautéed spinach, toasted pine nuts, a drizzle of olive oil, and a splash of vinegar for a delightful dish. Enjoy!

# Chili Lime Parsley Prawn Skewers

Prep time: 15 minutes | Cook time: 8 minutes | Serves 5

- ¼ cup fresh parsley leaves, minced
- 1 tablespoon garlic, crushed
- 2½ tablespoons olive oil
- 2 tablespoons Thai chili
- sauce
- 1 tablespoon fresh lime juice
- 1½ pounds (680 g) prawns, peeled and deveined

1. In a large bowl, combine all ingredients except for the prawns and mix well to create a flavorful marinade. 2. Place the marinade and the prawns into a resealable plastic bag. 3. Seal the bag tightly and shake it to ensure the prawns are well coated in the marinade. 4. Refrigerate the bag for about 20 to 30 minutes to allow the flavors to infuse. 5. Preheat the griddle to 450°F, preparing it for cooking. 6. Once marinated, remove the prawns from the bag and thread them onto metal skewers for easy grilling. 7. Arrange the skewers on the hot griddle and cook for about 4 minutes on each side, or until the prawns are pink and opaque. 8. Carefully remove the skewers from the griddle and serve hot for a delicious seafood dish. Enjoy!

# Caper Basil Halibut

Prep time: 10 minutes | Cook time: 8 minutes | Serves 4

- 24 ounces (680 g) halibut fillets
- 2 garlic cloves, crushed
- 2 tablespoons olive oil
- 2 teaspoons capers, drained
- 3 tablespoon fresh basil, sliced
- 2½ tablespoons fresh lemon juice

1. In a small bowl, whisk together minced garlic, olive oil, and lemon juice. Stir in 2 tablespoons of chopped basil to enhance the flavor. 2. Season the garlic mixture with pepper and salt to taste for added seasoning. 3. Season the fish fillets with pepper and salt, then brush them generously with the garlic mixture. 4. Preheat the griddle to high heat to prepare for cooking. 5. Once hot, place the fish fillets on the griddle and cook for 4 minutes on each side, or until they are golden brown and cooked through. 6. After cooking, transfer the fish fillets to a serving plate and top with the remaining garlic mixture and fresh basil for a burst of flavor. 7. Serve immediately and enjoy your delicious garlic and basil fish!

# Spicy Griddle Jumbo Shrimp

Prep time: 15 minutes | Cook time: 8 minutes | Serves 6

- 1½ pounds (680 g) uncooked jumbo shrimp, peeled and deveined

For the marinade:
- 2 tablespoons fresh parsley
- 1 bay leaf, dried
- 1 teaspoon chili powder
- 1 teaspoon garlic powder
- ¼ teaspoon cayenne pepper
- ¼ cup olive oil
- ¼ teaspoon salt
- ⅛ teaspoon pepper

1. In a food processor, combine all the marinade ingredients and blend until you achieve a smooth consistency. 2. Pour the marinade into a large mixing bowl, ready to add the shrimp. 3. Gently fold in the shrimp, ensuring each piece is well coated in the marinade. Cover the bowl and let it chill in the refrigerator for 30 minutes to enhance the flavors. 4. After marinating, carefully thread the shrimp onto metal skewers for grilling. 5. Preheat the griddle to medium heat, allowing it to reach the perfect temperature for cooking. 6. Place the shrimp skewers on the griddle and cook for 5 to 6 minutes, flipping them halfway through, until they turn opaque pink and are cooked through. 7. Once cooked, remove the skewers from the griddle and arrange them on a serving platter. Drizzle with a bit of fresh marinade for added flavor and garnish with lemon wedges. Enjoy your vibrant and flavorful shrimp skewers!

# Griddled Balsamic Glazed Salmon

- 6 salmon fillets
- 5 tablespoons balsamic vinaigrette
- 2 tablespoons olive oil
- 1½ teaspoons garlic powder
- Pepper
- Salt

1. In a mixing bowl, combine the salmon with garlic powder, balsamic vinaigrette, pepper, and salt, mixing well to ensure the salmon is evenly coated. Set the mixture aside to marinate for a few minutes. 2. Preheat the griddle to high heat, getting it ready for cooking. 3. Once hot, add a drizzle of oil to the griddle surface to prevent sticking. 4. Place the seasoned salmon onto the hot griddle and cook for 3 to 5 minutes on each side, or until the salmon is cooked through and flakes easily with a fork. 5. Once cooked, remove the salmon from the griddle and serve immediately. Enjoy your flavorful salmon dish!

# Oysters with Tequila Butter

- ½ teaspoon fennel seeds
- ¼ teaspoon crushed red pepper
- 7 tablespoon of unsalted butter
- ¼ cup of sage leaves, plus 36 small leaves for the garnish
- 1 teaspoon of dried oregano
- 2 tablespoons lemon juice
- 2 tablespoons of tequila
- Kosher salt
- rock salt, for the serving
- 3 douncesen scrubbed medium oysters

Intolerances:
- Gluten-Free
- Egg-Free
- Lactose-Free

1. On a griddle, toast the fennel seeds and crushed red pepper over moderate heat for about 1 minute, or until fragrant. 2. Transfer the toasted spices to a mortar and let them cool. Using a pestle, pound the spices into a coarse powder, then transfer them to a bowl. 3. In the same griddle, melt 3½ tablespoons of butter over moderate heat until it turns a dark color, which should take about 2 minutes. Add ¼ cup of sage leaves and continue cooking, occasionally turning the leaves, for about 2 minutes. Once done, move the sage to a plate and pour the browned butter into the bowl with the spices. Repeat the process with the remaining butter and sage, setting aside some fried sage leaves for garnish. 4. In the mortar, crush the fried sage leaves with the pestle. Add the crushed sage to the butter along with oregano, lemon juice, and tequila, then season with salt. Keep the sauce warm. 5. Preheat the griddle to high heat and line a platter with rock salt. Grill the oysters over high heat until they open, which should take about 1 to 2 minutes. 6. Discard the top shell and place the oysters on the rock salt, being careful not to spill their juices. Spoon the warm tequila sauce over each oyster, garnish with a fresh sage leaf, and serve immediately for a delightful seafood treat!

# Greek Salmon

- 12 ounces (340 g) salmon, cut into two pieces
- 1 teaspoon Greek seasoning
- 1 tablespoon olive oil
- ½ teaspoon lemon zest
- 1 garlic clove, minced
- Pepper - Salt

1. In a large bowl, combine olive oil, lemon zest, minced garlic, pepper, salt, and Greek seasoning to create a flavorful marinade. 2. Add the salmon fillets to the bowl and coat them well with the marinade. Set aside for 15 minutes to allow the flavors to infuse. 3. Preheat the griddle to high heat, preparing it for cooking. 4. Once hot, place the marinated salmon on the griddle and cook for 2 to 3 minutes. Flip the salmon to the other side and cook for an additional 2 to 3 minutes, or until the salmon is cooked through and flakes easily. 5. Once done, remove the salmon from the griddle and serve immediately. Enjoy your deliciously seasoned salmon!

# Grilled Salmon Steaks with Coconut Pineapple Shrimp Skewers

**Prep time: 1 hour 20 minutes | Cook time:5 minutes | Serves 4**

- 1½ pounds (680 g) uncooked jumbo shrimp, peeled and deveined
- ½ cup light coconut milk
- 1 tablespoon cilantro, chopped
- 4 teaspoons Tabasco Original Red Sauce
- 2 teaspoons soy sauce
- ¼ cup freshly squeezed orange juice
- ¼ cup freshly squeezed lime juice (from about 2 large limes)
- ¾ pounds (340 g) pineapple, cut into 1 inch chunks
- Olive oil, for griddleing

1. In a mixing bowl, combine coconut milk, chopped cilantro, Tabasco sauce, soy sauce, orange juice, and lime juice. Add the shrimp and toss well to ensure they are fully coated in the marinade. 2. Cover the bowl and refrigerate for 1 hour to allow the flavors to meld. 3. After marinating, thread the shrimp and pineapple onto metal skewers, alternating between the two for a delicious combination. 4. Preheat the griddle to medium heat, preparing it for cooking. 5. Place the skewers on the griddle and cook for 5 to 6 minutes, flipping them once, until the shrimp turn an opaque pink color and are cooked through. 6. Once done, serve the skewers immediately for a delightful meal! Enjoy!

# Citrus Soy Squid

**Prep time: 15 minutes | Cook time: 45 minutes | Serves 4**

- 1 cup mirin
- 1 cup of soy sauce
- ⅓ cup yuzu juice or fresh lemon juice
- 2 cups of water
- 2 pounds ( 0.9 kg) squid tentacles left whole; bodies cut crosswise 1 inch thick

Intolerances:
- Gluten-Free
- Egg-Free
- Lactose-Free

1. In a bowl, combine the mirin, soy sauce, yuzu juice, and water to create a flavorful marinade. 2. Set aside a small amount of the marinade in a container and refrigerate it for later use. 3. Add the squid to the bowl with the remaining marinade and let it sit for about 30 minutes, or refrigerate for up to 4 hours for a deeper flavor. 4. Preheat the griddle to medium-high heat. Once ready, drain the squid from the marinade. 5. Place the squid on the griddle and cook for about 3 minutes, turning once, until it is opaque and cooked through. 6. Remove from the griddle and serve hot for a delicious seafood dish! Enjoy!

# Griddled Sea Scallops with Fresh Corn Salad

**Prep time: 25 minutes | Cook time: 30 minutes | Serves 6**

- 6 shucked ears of corn
- 1-pint grape tomatoes, halved
- 3 sliced scallions, white and light green parts only
- ⅓ cup basil leaves, finely shredded
- Salt and grounded pepper
- 1 small shallot, minced
- 2 tablespoons balsamic vinegar
- 2 tablespoons hot water
- 1 teaspoon Dijon mustard ¼ cup
- 3 tablespoon sunflower oil
- 1½ pounds (680 g) sea scallops

Intolerances:
- Gluten-Free
- Egg-Free
- Lactose-Free

1. Bring a pot of salted water to a boil and cook the corn for about 5 minutes. Once done, drain the corn and let it cool. 2. In a large bowl, cut the kernels off the cooled corn and add diced tomatoes, sliced scallions, and chopped basil. Season the mixture with salt and freshly ground pepper to taste. 3. In a blender, combine minced shallot, vinegar, heated water, and mustard. While blending, gradually add 6 tablespoons of sunflower oil until the dressing is emulsified. 4. Season the vinaigrette with additional salt and pepper, then pour it over the corn salad and mix well. 5. In a separate bowl, toss the scallops with the remaining 1 tablespoon of oil, and season with salt and freshly ground pepper. 6. Preheat a griddle pan over high heat. Add half of the scallops and grill for about 4 minutes, turning them once, until they are nicely seared. 7. Remove the first batch and repeat with the remaining scallops. 8. To serve, place a generous portion of corn salad on each plate and top with the seared scallops. Enjoy your delicious meal!

# Chapter
# 5

# Poultry

# Chapter 5 Poultry

## Chicken Parmesan With Grilled Tomato Sauce

**Prep time: 10 minutes | Cook time:15 minutes | Serves 2**

- 2 eggs
- ¼ cup water
- 2 cups all-purpose flour
- 1 tablespoon salt
- 1 tablespoon pepper
- 1 tablespoon garlic powder
- 1 tablespoon onion powder
- 1 tablespoon dried oregano
- 2 cups panko bread crumbs
- 2 boneless, skinless chicken breasts, tenderloins removed
- very thinly sliced basil, for garnish
- ½ cup shredded mozzarella

- cheese, to serve
- cooking oil or butter, as needed
- Marinara sauce
- 2 cups diced canned tomatoes
- 1 tablespoon tomato paste
- 1 teaspoon minced garlic
- water, as needed
- 1 teaspoon garlic powder
- 1 teaspoon salt
- 1 teaspoon dried basil
- 1 teaspoon dried oregano
- pinch of sugar
- cooking oil, as needed

1. In a large, shallow bowl, beat the eggs with water until well mixed. In another large, shallow dish, combine flour, salt, pepper, garlic powder, onion powder, and oregano. In a third dish, place the bread crumbs. 2. Pound the chicken breasts to an even thickness of about ½ inch, then pat them dry with paper towels. Arrange your breading stations in an assembly line: flour/herb mixture, egg wash, and bread crumbs. Dip each chicken piece into the seasoned flour, flipping multiple times to ensure an even, thin coating. Next, dredge the floured chicken in the egg wash on both sides until evenly covered. Finally, coat the chicken in the bread crumbs, flipping two or three times to form a shell around the meat. If there are any bald spots, return those areas to the egg wash and then back into the bread crumbs. Repeat this process for the remaining chicken breasts, and place them on a dry plate in the refrigerator, uncovered, for 30 minutes. 3. For the marinara sauce, preheat the griddle grill to medium heat (about 325°F). Lightly coat the surface with cooking oil or butter. Sauté the diced tomatoes and garlic for 5 to 7 minutes, allowing the tomatoes to break down and soften without excessive browning. Transfer the mixture to a blender, adding the remaining sauce ingredients. Blend at low speed for about a minute, then gradually increase the speed until the sauce is completely

smooth. If the sauce is too thick, add water one tablespoon at a time until you reach the desired consistency. 4. Clean the griddle thoroughly after sautéing the tomatoes, then reheat it to about 375°F. Coat the griddle with a moderate amount of oil. Once the oil begins to shimmer, place the breaded chicken breasts on the hot griddle. Allow them to cook undisturbed for 2 to 3 minutes to help the breading adhere. Add more oil around the chicken as needed. When the oil shimmers, flip the chicken to the uncooked side and cover. Cook for 3 to 5 minutes, covered, without disturbance. After removing the lid, flip the chicken again, adding more oil if necessary. Cook until the internal temperature reaches a safe 165°F. 5. For the finishing touches, flip the chicken one last time and spoon about ½ cup of marinara sauce over each piece, or enough to your liking. Top the chicken and sauce with mozzarella cheese. To melt the cheese, add a small amount of water to the griddle around the chicken, then cover immediately to capture the steam. A little water on the side of the chicken is fine, but avoid soaking the breaded crust to keep it crispy. Finally, serve the chicken garnished with ribbons of freshly sliced basil for added flavor and presentation. Enjoy your delicious dish!

## Chicken BBQ with Sweet And Sour Sauce

**Prep time: 5 minutes | Cook time: 40 minutes | Serves 6**

- ¼ cup minced garlic
- ¼ cup tomato paste
- ¾ cup minced onion
- ¾ cup sugar
- 1 cup soy sauce

- 1 cup water
- 1 cup white vinegar
- chicken drumsticks
- Salt and pepper to taste

1. In a Ziploc bag, combine all ingredients to create a marinade for the chicken. 2. Seal the bag and allow the chicken to marinate in the refrigerator for at least 2 hours to enhance the flavor. 3. Preheat the griddle to high heat. Once hot, place the chicken on the griddle and cook for 40 minutes. 4. Flip the chicken every 10 minutes to ensure even cooking and browning on all sides. 5. While the chicken is cooking, pour the marinade into a saucepan and heat it over medium flame until it thickens into a glaze. 6. Before serving, brush the cooked chicken with the thickened glaze for added flavor and shine. Enjoy your deliciously marinated and glazed chicken!

# Griddled Rosemary Butter Cornish Hen

**Prep time: 10 minutes | Cook time: 1 hour | Serves 2**

- 1 cornish hen, rinse and pat dry with paper towels
- 1 tablespoon butter, melted
- 1 rosemary sprigs
- 1 teaspoon poultry seasoning

1. Begin by stuffing fresh rosemary sprigs into the cavity of the Cornish hen for added flavor. 2. Brush the hen generously with melted butter, then season it evenly with poultry seasoning to enhance the taste. 3. Preheat the griddle to high heat, allowing it to reach the ideal cooking temperature. 4. Lightly spray the griddle surface with cooking spray to prevent sticking. 5. Place the hen on the hot griddle and cook for about 60 minutes, or until the internal temperature of the hen reaches 165°F, ensuring it is cooked through. 6. Once cooked, carefully remove the hen from the griddle and let it rest for a few minutes. Slice it up and serve warm, perhaps with your favorite sides for a delightful meal. Enjoy your savory rosemary-infused hen!

# Chicken "steaks"

**Prep time: 5 minutes | Cook time: 8 minutes | Serves 4**

- 2 whole boneless chicken breasts (each 12 to 16 ounces / 340 g-453 g), or 4 half chicken breasts (each half 6 to 8 ounces / 227 g)
- Coarse salt (kosher or sea) and freshly ground black pepper
- ¼ cup white wine vinegar or red wine vinegar
- ½ sweet onion, finely diced (about ½ cup)
- 3 cloves garlic, coarsely chopped
- 1 teaspoon dried oregano
- ½ teaspoon ground cumin
- ¾ cup extra-virgin olive oil
- ⅓ cup chopped fresh flat-leaf parsley

1. If you're using whole chicken breasts, cut each breast in half and remove the tenders. Place each breast half between two pieces of plastic wrap and gently pound it to a thickness of ½ inch using a meat pounder, the side of a heavy cleaver, a rolling pin, or the bottom of a heavy saucepan. Repeat this process with the remaining breast halves. Once finished, place the chicken breasts in a large baking dish and season both sides generously with salt and pepper. 2. In a nonreactive mixing bowl, combine vinegar, diced onion, minced garlic, oregano, and cumin. Add ½ teaspoon of salt and ¼ teaspoon of pepper, whisking until the salt dissolves. Slowly whisk in the olive oil, and taste to adjust the seasoning; the mixture should be robustly seasoned. Pour half of this marinade into another nonreactive serving bowl and set it aside for later use as

a sauce. Add 2 tablespoons of chopped parsley to the marinade in the mixing bowl and pour it over the chicken, turning the breasts to ensure they are well coated on both sides. Cover and let the chicken marinate in the refrigerator for at least 2 hours, or overnight if possible, turning occasionally for even flavor absorption. 3. When ready to cook, drain the chicken breasts well and discard the marinade. 4. Turn the control knob to the high position on your griddle. Once the griddle is hot, place the chicken breasts on it and cook for about 5 minutes. To check for doneness, use the poke test: the chicken should feel firm when pressed. Alternatively, insert an instant-read meat thermometer into the thickest part of the breast; it should read about 160°F. Depending on your griddle size, you may need to cook the chicken in batches. Keep the cooked chicken warm by covering it with aluminum foil until you're ready to serve. 5. Finally, whisk the remaining parsley into the reserved vinegar mixture. Spoon half of it over the cooked chicken breasts and serve the remainder on the side for dipping. Enjoy your flavorful dish!

# Ginger-Lemon Smoked Chicken

**Prep time: 30 minutes | Cook time: 6 hours | Serves 1**

Ingredients:
- 2 (4 pounds / 1.8 kg) whole chicken
- ¼ cup olive oil

For the rub
- ¼ cup salt
- 2 tablespoons pepper
- ¼ cup garlic powder

For the filling
- 8, 1-inch each fresh ginger
- 8 cinnamon sticks
- ½ cup sliced lemon
- 6 cloves

For the smoke
- Preheat the griddle an hour prior to smoking.

1. Preheat your griddle to 225°F (107°C) to prepare for smoking the chicken. 2. Generously rub the chicken with salt, pepper, and garlic powder, then set it aside to allow the seasoning to penetrate. 3. Stuff the cavities of the chicken with ginger, cinnamon sticks, whole cloves, and slices of lemon. After stuffing, brush olive oil all over the exterior of the chicken for added flavor and moisture. 4. Once the griddle reaches the desired temperature, carefully place the whole chicken on the griddle's rack. 5. Smoke the chicken for approximately 4 hours, checking periodically until the internal temperature reaches 160°F (71°C) to ensure it's fully cooked. 6. When the chicken is finished smoking, carefully remove it from the griddle and let it rest for a few minutes to retain its juices. 7. Serve the chicken warm, enjoying it as is or slicing it into portions for sharing. Enjoy your deliciously smoked chicken!

# Garlic Parmesan Grilled Cheese Sandwiches

**Prep time: 2 minutes | Cook time: 7 minutes | Serves 1**

- 2 slices Italian bread, sliced thin
- 2 slices provolone cheese
- 2 tablespoons butter, softened
- Garlic powder, for dusting
- Dried parsley, for dusting
- Parmesan Cheese, shredded, for dusting

1. Begin by spreading a generous layer of butter on two slices of bread. Evenly sprinkle the buttered sides with minced garlic and fresh parsley for added flavor. 2. Next, sprinkle a few tablespoons of Parmesan cheese over each buttered side and gently press the cheese into the bread to ensure it adheres well. 3. Preheat the griddle to medium heat, preparing it for cooking. Once hot, place one slice of bread, buttered side down, onto the griddle. 4. Layer slices of provolone cheese on top of the bread, then place the second slice of bread on top, buttered side facing up. 5. Cook the sandwich for about 3 minutes, then carefully flip it over to cook for another 3 minutes on the other side. Continue cooking until the bread is golden brown and the Parmesan cheese is crispy. 6. Once done, remove the sandwich from the griddle and serve it warm with your favorite sides for a delicious meal! Enjoy your cheesy delight!

# Slow-Grilled Shawarma Feast

**Prep time: 30 minutes | Cook time: 4 hours | Serves 1**

- 5½ pounds (2.5 kg) of chicken thighs; boneless, skinless
- 4½ pounds (2.04 kg) of lamb fat
- Pita bread
- 5½ pounds (2.5 kg) of top
- sirloin
- 2 yellow onions; large
- 4 tablespoons of rub
- Desired toppings like pickles, tomatoes, fries, salad and more

1. Begin by slicing the meat and fat into ½-inch thick slices and placing them in three separate bowls. 2. Season each bowl with the spice rub, then massage the rub into the meat to ensure it seeps in well for maximum flavor. 3. At the base of each half skewer, place half of an onion to create a firm foundation for the skewers. 4. Alternate adding two layers of meat from each of the bowls onto the skewers at a time, ensuring to maintain a symmetrical arrangement. 5. Once the skewers are filled, place the other half of the onions on top to complete the assembly. 6. Wrap the assembled skewers in plastic wrap and refrigerate them overnight to enhance the flavors. 7. When ready to cook, preheat the griddle to 275°F. 8. Lay the shawarma skewers on the griddle grate and allow them to cook for approximately 4 hours, making sure to turn them at least once for even cooking. 9. After 4 hours, remove the skewers from the griddle and increase the temperature to 445°F. 10. Place a cast iron griddle on the griddle grate and add a drizzle of olive oil. 11. Once the cast iron is hot, place the whole shawarma on it and smoke for 5 to 10 minutes on each side to achieve a nice sear. 12. Remove the shawarma from the griddle and slice off the edges for serving. 13. Repeat the same cooking process with any leftover shawarma. 14. Serve the shawarma in pita bread with your choice of toppings. Enjoy your delicious homemade shawarma!

# Smoky Tabasco-Glazed Turkey

**Prep time: 20 minutes | Cook time: 4 hours 15 minutes | Serves 8**

- 4 pounds (1.8 kg)whole turkey
- For the rub
- ¼ cup brown sugar
- 2 teaspoons smoked paprika
- 1 teaspoon salt
- 1½ teaspoons onion powder
- 2 teaspoons oregano
- 2 teaspoons garlic powder
- ½ teaspoon dried thyme
- ½ teaspoon white pepper
- ½ teaspoon cayenne pepper
- The Glaze
- ½ cup ketchup
- ½ cup hot sauce
- 1 tablespoon cider vinegar
- 2 teaspoons tabasco
- ½ teaspoon cajun spices
- 3 tablespoons unsalted butter

1. Rub the turkey thoroughly with 2 tablespoons of brown sugar, smoked paprika, salt, onion powder, garlic powder, dried thyme, white pepper, and cayenne pepper. Allow the turkey to rest for 1 hour to let the flavors meld. 2. Set the griddle for indirect heat and adjust the temperature to 275°F (135°C) to prepare for smoking. 3. Place the seasoned turkey on the griddle and smoke it for 4 hours, maintaining a consistent temperature. 4. Meanwhile, in a saucepan, combine ketchup, hot sauce, cider vinegar, Tabasco, and Cajun spices. Bring the mixture to a simmer over medium heat. 5. Once simmering, remove the sauce from the heat and quickly add unsalted butter, stirring until fully melted and combined. 6. After 4 hours of smoking, baste the turkey generously with the Tabasco sauce, then continue to smoke for an additional 15 minutes. 7. When the internal temperature of the smoked turkey reaches 170°F (77°C), remove it from the griddle and transfer it to a serving dish. Enjoy your flavorful smoked turkey!

# Turkey Jerky

Marinade:
- 1 cup pineapple juice
- ½ cup brown sugar
- 2 tablespoons sriracha
- 2 teaspoons onion powder
- 2 tablespoons minced garlic
- 2 tablespoons rice wine vinegar
- 2 tablespoons hoisin
- 1 tablespoon red pepper flakes
- 1 tablespoon coarsely ground black pepper flakes
- 2 cups coconut amino
- 2 jalapenos (thinly sliced)

Meat:
- 3 pounds (1.36 kg) turkey boneless skinless breasts (sliced to ¼ inch thick)

1. In a container, combine the marinade ingredients and mix until well blended. Place the turkey slices in a gallon-sized ziplock bag and pour the marinade over the turkey. Massage the marinade into the meat to ensure it's evenly coated. Seal the bag and refrigerate for 8 hours to allow the flavors to penetrate. 2. After marinating, remove the turkey slices from the marinade and pat them dry with a paper towel to remove excess liquid. 3. Activate the griddle for smoking by turning it on and letting it heat up for 5 minutes until the fire starts. 4. Close the lid and preheat your griddle to 180°F. 5. Once preheated, arrange the turkey slices on the griddle in a single layer. 6. Smoke the turkey for about 3 to 4 hours, turning the slices often after the first 2 hours of smoking. The jerky should appear dark and dry when it's fully cooked. 7. Once done, remove the jerky from the griddle and let it cool for about 1 hour. You can serve it immediately or store it in the refrigerator for later enjoyment. Enjoy your homemade turkey jerky!

# Five-Spice Griddled Cornish Hen

- 1 cornish hen
- 1½ teaspoons Chinese five-spice powder
- 1½ teaspoons rice wine
- ½ teaspoon pepper
- 2 cups of water
- 3 tablespoons soy sauce
- 2 tablespoons sugar
- Salt

1. In a large mixing bowl, combine water, soy sauce, sugar, rice wine, five-spice powder, pepper, and salt, stirring well until the sugar dissolves completely. 2. Submerge the Cornish hen in the marinade, ensuring it's fully coated, then cover the bowl and refrigerate it overnight to enhance the flavors. 3. When ready to cook, preheat the griddle to high heat, allowing it to get nice and hot. 4. Lightly spray the griddle surface with cooking spray to prevent sticking. 5. Carefully remove the Cornish hen from the marinade and place it on the hot griddle. Cook for about 60 minutes, flipping occasionally, or until the internal temperature of the hen reaches 185°F for perfect doneness. 6. Once cooked, transfer the Cornish hen to a cutting board and let it rest for a few minutes before slicing. Serve it warm, garnished with your choice of herbs or side dishes, for a delightful meal. Enjoy your flavorful creation!

# Smoked Turkey Breast

For The Brine
- 1 cup of kosher salt
- 1 cup of maple syrup
- ¼ cup of brown sugar
- ¼ cup of whole black peppercorns
- 4 cups of cold bourbon
- 1½ gallons of cold water
- 1 turkey breast of about 7 pounds (3.2 kg)

For The Turkey
- 3 tablespoons of brown sugar
- 1½ tablespoons of smoked paprika
- 1½ teaspoons of chipotle chili powder
- 1½ teaspoons of garlic powder
- 1½ teaspoons of salt
- 1½ teaspoons of black pepper
- 1 teaspoon of onion powder
- ½ teaspoon of ground cumin
- 6 tablespoons of melted unsalted butter

1. Before starting, ensure that the bourbon, water, and chicken stock are all cold for effective brining. 2. To make the brine, combine salt, syrup, sugar, peppercorns, bourbon, and water in a large bucket, stirring well until everything is fully dissolved. 3. Remove any leftover parts from the turkey, such as the neck and giblets, to prepare it for brining. 4. Place the turkey in a resealable bag and pour the brine over it, ensuring it's fully submerged. Refrigerate for about 8 to 12 hours for optimal flavor. 5. After brining, take the turkey breast out and pat it dry with clean paper towels. Place it on a baking sheet and refrigerate for about 1 hour to allow the surface to dry. 6. Preheat your griddle to around 300°F, getting it ready for cooking. 7. In a bowl, mix paprika, sugar, chili powder, garlic powder, salt, pepper, onion powder, and cumin, ensuring the spices are well combined. 8. Carefully lift the skin of the turkey breast and rub melted butter directly onto the meat for added moisture and flavor. 9. Generously apply the spice mixture over the meat and under the skin, ensuring even coverage. 10. Smoke the turkey breast for approximately 1½ hours at a temperature of about 375°F, or until it reaches the desired internal temperature. Enjoy your flavorful, smoked turkey!

# Savory Chicken Burgers

Prep time: 10 minutes | Cook time: 20 minutes | Serves 3

- 1 pound (454 g) ground chicken
- ½ red onion, finely chopped
- 1 teaspoon garlic powder
- ½ teaspoon onion powder
- ¼ teaspoon black pepper
- ½ teaspoon salt
- 3 tablespoons vegetable oil
- 3 potato buns, toasted

1. In a large bowl, combine ground chicken, diced onion, garlic powder, onion powder, pepper, and salt. Mix gently until all ingredients are well incorporated, being careful not to overwork the mixture to keep the patties tender. Form the mixture into three equal-sized patties. 2. Preheat your griddle to medium-high heat and add a drizzle of vegetable oil, allowing it to heat until shimmering. 3. Once the oil is hot, carefully add the chicken patties to the griddle and cook for about 5 minutes on each side, or until the internal temperature of the patties reaches 165°F. 4. After cooking, remove the patties from the griddle and let them rest for five minutes to allow the juices to redistribute. Serve the patties on toasted buns for a delicious meal! Enjoy!

# Ranch Turkey Burgers with Mozzarella

Prep time: 8 minutes | Cook time: 10 minutes | Serves 4

- 1 pound (454g) ground turkey
- 1 egg
- ¼ cup powdered ranch seasoning
- ¼ cup mozzarella crumbles
- ¼ cup seasoned bread crumbs
- 4 burger buns
- butter, as needed
- cooking oil, as needed

1. In a mixing bowl, combine ground turkey, egg, ranch seasoning, mozzarella crumbles, and bread crumbs. Mix until everything is well incorporated. Divide the mixture into four equal patties and set aside. 2. Preheat the griddle to medium-high heat. Add enough butter to the griddle to coat the surface, and then place the burger buns on the griddle. Cook for 2 to 3 minutes, or until the buns are golden brown and warmed. Remove and set aside. 3. Lightly coat the griddle with cooking oil. Place the turkey patties on the griddle and cook them, covered, for 4 to 6 minutes on each side, or until the internal temperature of the turkey reaches at least 165°F. 4. Once cooked, serve the turkey burgers on the warmed buns for a delicious meal! Enjoy!

# Grilled Chicken Yakitori with Sweet Ginger Sauce

Prep time: 10 minutes | Cook time:20 minutes | Serves 8

- ½ cup water
- ¼ cup cornstarch
- 2 pounds (907g) boneless, skinless chicken thighs, cut into 1-inch cubes
- 2 cloves garlic, minced
- 2 tablespoons soy sauce or tamari sauce

Sauce:
- ½ cup soy sauce or tamari sauce
- ½ cup low-sodium chicken broth
- 2 tablespoons rice wine vinegar

- 1 tablespoon black pepper
- 2 tablespoons freshly grated ginger
- 1 tablespoon sesame oil
- cooking oil, as needed
- sesame seeds, for garnish
- finely chopped green onion, for garnish

- 2 tablespoons mirin
- ½ cup brown sugar
- 2 tablespoons honey
- 2 tablespoons freshly grated ginger
- 3 cloves garlic, minced

1. In a medium bowl, whisk together water and cornstarch until smooth, ensuring there are no lumps. Divide the mixture in half for later use. 2. Marinate the chicken in one half of the cornstarch slurry, adding garlic, soy sauce (or tamari), black pepper, ginger, and sesame oil. Cover and refrigerate for 30 minutes to 4 hours to allow the flavors to develop. 3. While the chicken is marinating, combine the sauce ingredients in a saucepan and heat over medium-high on the stovetop. Bring to a gentle boil, stirring frequently to dissolve the sugar. Let it boil for about 3 minutes, then remove from heat and stir in the remaining half of the cornstarch slurry. Return to medium heat, stirring until the sauce reaches a slow boil again. Allow it to simmer for an additional 90 seconds or until thick enough to coat the back of a spoon. Divide the sauce in half and set aside. 4. Preheat the griddle to medium-high heat. Skewer the marinated chicken cubes closely together on metal skewers, discarding any leftover marinade. 5. Generously oil the grill and cook the chicken skewers for 8 to 12 minutes, covered, turning them a quarter turn every couple of minutes for even cooking. If the chicken begins to brown too quickly, squirt a little water onto the grilling surface and skewers to create steam and help with cooking. 6. Brush half of the prepared sauce onto the chicken skewers, allowing it to reduce and coat the meat. Be mindful of the griddle temperature to prevent the marinade from burning. Apply the sauce in layers to create a rich coating on the chicken. Remove the skewers once the internal temperature of the chicken reaches 165°F. 7. Garnish the chicken with sesame seeds and chopped green onions. Serve with the remaining sauce on the side for dipping. Enjoy your delicious chicken skewers!

# Seared Chicken with Tropical Fruit Salsa

**Prep time: 1 hour | Cook time: 20 minutes | Serves 4**

* 4 boneless, skinless chicken breasts

For the marinade:

* ½ cup fresh lemon juice
* ½ cup soy sauce
* 1 tablespoon fresh ginger, minced
* 1 tablespoon lemon pepper seasoning
* 2 garlic cloves, minced

For the salsa:

* 1½ cups pineapple, chopped
* ¾ cup kiwi fruit, chopped
* ½ cup mango, chopped
* ½ cup red onion, finely chopped
* 2 tablespoons fresh cilantro, chopped
* 1 small jalapeño pepper, seeded and chopped
* 1½ teaspoons ground cumin
* ¼ teaspoon sea salt
* ⅛ teaspoon black pepper
* ½ teaspoon olive oil, more for brushing griddle

1. In a large sealable plastic bag, combine all the marinade ingredients. 2. Add the chicken to the bag, seal it tightly, and toss to ensure the chicken is evenly coated. Allow it to marinate in the refrigerator for 1 hour for maximum flavor. 3. While the chicken is marinating, prepare the salsa by combining all the salsa ingredients in a mixing bowl. Toss gently to mix and set aside until you're ready to serve. 4. Preheat the griddle to medium heat to prepare for cooking. 5. After marinating, remove the chicken from the bag and discard the marinade. 6. Brush the griddle with olive oil and place the chicken on it, cooking for 7 minutes on each side, or until the chicken is fully cooked through and no longer pink. 7. Once cooked, serve the chicken topped with the prepared salsa and enjoy alongside your favorite side dishes for a delicious meal!

# Italian-Style Sweet Pork Sausage with Fennel Seeds

**Prep time: 5 minutes | Cook time: 10 minutes | Serves 8**

* 2½ pounds (1.13 kg) fatty boneless pork shoulder, cut into 1-inch cubes
* 3 cloves garlic, minced
* 1 tablespoon fennel seeds
* 1 teaspoon salt
* 1 teaspoon black pepper
* Sausage casings (optional)

1. In batches, place the meat in a food processor and pulse until it's coarsely ground—finer than chopped but not overly pulverized.

Take your time to ensure the texture is just right. Once each batch is finished, transfer it to a bowl. Add minced garlic, fennel seeds, salt, and pepper, and gently work the mixture with your hands to combine. If the mixture seems dry or crumbly, add a little water to help bind it. To taste for seasoning, cook a small spoonful in a small griddle; adjust seasoning as needed. Shape the mixture into 8 or more patties, or stuff into casings if you prefer sausage links. You can freeze some or all of the patties, wrapped well, for up to several months. 2. Preheat the griddle to high heat. Once the griddle is hot, place the sausages or patties on the surface. Cook until they easily release from the grates, about 5 to 10 minutes. Turn them over and continue cooking until they are no longer pink in the center, ensuring the internal temperature reaches 160°F (check with an instant-read thermometer or cut into one to peek inside). Transfer the cooked sausages to a platter and serve hot. Enjoy your homemade sausages!

# Seared Chicken Kale Caesar Salad

**Prep time: 10 minutes | Cook time: 8 minutes | Serves 1**

* 1 chicken breast
* 1 teaspoon garlic powder
* ½ teaspoon black pepper
* ½ teaspoon sea salt
* 2 kale leaves, chopped
* shaved parmesan, for serving

For the dressing:

* 1 tablespoon mayonnaise
* ½ tablespoon dijon mustard
* ½ teaspoon garlic powder
* ½ teaspoon worcestershire sauce
* ¼ lemon, juice of (or ½ a small lime)
* ¼ teaspoon anchovy paste
* Pinch of sea salt
* Pinch of black pepper

1. In a small mixing bowl, combine garlic powder, black pepper, and sea salt to create a seasoning mix. Coat the chicken evenly with this mixture to enhance its flavor. 2. Preheat the griddle to medium-high heat to prepare for cooking the chicken. 3. Once hot, sear the chicken on each side for about 7 minutes, or until the internal temperature reaches 165°F (74°C) when checked with a meat thermometer inserted into the thickest part of the breast. 4. While the chicken is cooking, whisk together all of the dressing ingredients in a separate bowl until well combined. 5. Place your kale on a serving plate and pour the dressing over it, tossing to ensure the kale is evenly coated. 6. After the chicken is cooked, cut it diagonally into slices and arrange it on top of the dressed kale. Garnish with shaved Parmesan cheese, and serve immediately for a delicious and nutritious meal! Enjoy!

# Spiced Lemon Chicken

**Prep time: 30 minutes | Cook time: 5 hours | Serves 1**

- 1 whole chicken
- 4 cloves of minced garlic
- Zest of 2 fresh lemons
- 1 tablespoon of olive oil
- 1 tablespoon of smoked paprika
- 1½ teaspoons of salt
- ½ teaspoon of black pepper
- ½ teaspoon of dried oregano
- 1 tablespoon of ground cumin

1. Preheat the griddle to 375°F to prepare for cooking the chicken. 2. To spatchcock the chicken, use kitchen shears to cut along both sides of the backbone, from the neck to the tail. Remove the backbone completely. 3. Lay the chicken flat and press down firmly on the breastbone to break the ribs and flatten the bird. 4. In a bowl, combine all leftover ingredients (except for ½ teaspoon of salt) and crush them together to create a smooth rub. 5. Generously spread the rub all over the chicken, making sure to get it under the skin for maximum flavor. 6. Place the prepared chicken on the griddle grates and cook for about 1 hour, or until the internal temperature reaches 165°F. 7. Once cooked, remove the chicken from the griddle and let it rest for 10 minutes to allow the juices to redistribute. 8. Serve the chicken warm and enjoy your deliciously spatchcocked meal!

# Griddled Salsa Verde Chicken

**Prep time: 4 hours 35 minutes | Cook time: 4 hours 50 minutes | Serves 6**

- 6 boneless, skinless chicken breasts
- 1 tablespoon olive oil
- 1 teaspoon sea salt

For the salsa verde marinade:

- 3 teaspoons garlic, minced
- 1 small onion, chopped
- 6 tomatillos, husked, rinsed and chopped
- 1 medium jalapeño pepper,
- 1 teaspoon chili powder
- 1 teaspoon ground cumin
- 1 teaspoon garlic powder

 

    cut in half, seeded
- ¼ cup fresh cilantro, chopped
- ½ teaspoon sugar or sugar substitute

1. Begin by adding the salsa verde marinade ingredients to a food processor and pulse until smooth and well blended. 2. In a small mixing bowl, combine sea salt, chili powder, cumin, and garlic powder to create a seasoning mix. Rub the chicken breasts with olive oil and then coat them evenly with the seasoning mix. Place the seasoned chicken in a glass baking dish. 3. Spread a tablespoon of the salsa verde marinade over each chicken breast, ensuring they

are fully covered. Reserve the remaining salsa for serving later. 4. Cover the baking dish with plastic wrap and refrigerate for 4 hours to allow the flavors to penetrate the chicken. 5. When you're ready to cook, preheat the griddle to medium-high heat and brush the surface with olive oil to prevent sticking. 6. Place the marinated chicken breasts on the griddle and cook for 7 minutes on each side, or until the juices run clear and a meat thermometer inserted into the thickest part reads 165°F (74°C). 7. Once cooked, serve each chicken breast with additional salsa verde on top and enjoy your flavorful meal!

# Chicken Fajitas

**Prep time: 10 minutes | Cook time: 15 minutes | Serves 4**

- boneless, skinless chicken breasts, sliced
- small red onion, sliced
- red bell peppers, sliced
- ½ cup spicy ranch salad dressing, divided
- ½ teaspoon dried oregano
- 8 corn tortillas
- 1 cups torn butter lettuce
- avocados, peeled and chopped

1. In a bowl, combine the chicken, diced onion, and sliced pepper. Drizzle with 1 tablespoon of the salad dressing and sprinkle in the oregano. Toss everything together to ensure an even coating. 2. Preheat the griddle to high heat. Once hot, add the chicken and cook for 10 to 14 minutes, or until the internal temperature reaches 165°F as measured by a food thermometer. 3. Once the chicken is cooked, transfer it along with the vegetables to a bowl and toss with the remaining salad dressing for added flavor. 4. Serve the chicken and vegetable mixture alongside tortillas, fresh lettuce, and sliced avocados, allowing everyone to assemble their own creations as desired. Enjoy your delicious and customizable meal!

# BBQ Hen

**Prep time: 10 minutes | Cook time: 1 hour 30 minutes | Serves 8**

- 1 cornish hen
- 2 tablespoons BBQ rub

1. Preheat the griddle to high heat to prepare for cooking the hens. 2. Lightly spray the griddle surface with cooking spray to prevent sticking. 3. Generously coat the hens with BBQ rub, ensuring they are well seasoned. Place the seasoned hens on the hot griddle and cook for approximately 1½ hours, or until the internal temperature reaches 165°F. 4. Once cooked, remove the hens from the griddle, slice them up, and serve immediately for a delicious meal! Enjoy!

# Balsamic-Rosemary Chicken Breasts

**Prep time: 5 minutes | Cook time: 6 minutes | Serves 4**

½ cup balsamic vinegar
2 tablespoons olive oil
2 rosemary sprigs, coarsely chopped
2 pounds ( 0.9 kg) boneless, skinless chicken breasts, pounded to
½-inch thickness

1. In a shallow baking dish, combine balsamic vinegar, olive oil, and chopped rosemary. 2. Add the chicken breasts to the dish, turning them to coat thoroughly in the marinade. Cover the dish with plastic wrap and refrigerate for at least 30 minutes, or ideally overnight, to enhance the flavor. 3. Preheat the griddle to high heat. Once the griddle is hot, place the marinated chicken breasts on it. Cook for about 6 minutes, or until the chicken has developed nice griddle marks and is fully cooked through. Enjoy your deliciously marinated chicken!

# Marinated Smoked Turkey Breast

**Prep time: 15 minutes | Cook time: 4 hours | Serves 6**

- 1 (5 pounds / 2.3 kg) boneless chicken breast
- 4 cups water
- 2 tablespoons kosher salt

For the rub:
- ½ teaspoon onion powder
- 1 teaspoon paprika
- 1 teaspoon salt
- 1 teaspoon ground black

- 1 teaspoon Italian seasoning
- 2 tablespoons honey
- 1 tablespoon cider vinegar

pepper
- 1 tablespoon brown sugar
- ½ teaspoon garlic powder
- 1 teaspoon oregano

1. In a large container, mix together water, honey, cider vinegar, Italian seasoning, and salt until well combined. 2. Add the chicken breasts to the mixture and toss to coat. Cover the bowl and refrigerate for 4 hours to allow the flavors to infuse. 3. After marinating, rinse the chicken breasts under water and pat them dry with paper towels. 4. In a separate mixing bowl, combine brown sugar, salt, paprika, onion powder, pepper, oregano, and garlic powder to create a seasoning rub. 5. Generously season the chicken breasts with the rub, ensuring they are well coated. 6. Preheat the griddle to 225°F with the lid closed for about 15 minutes. 7. Place the seasoned chicken breasts on a griddle rack and set the rack on the griddle. 8. Smoke the chicken for approximately 3 to 4 hours, or until the internal temperature reaches 165°F. 9. Once cooked,

remove the chicken breasts from the heat and let them rest for a few minutes before serving. Enjoy your deliciously smoked chicken!

# Apple-Brined Cornish Hen

**Prep time: 10 minutes | Cook time: 60 minutes | Serves 2**

- 1 cornish hen
- 1 cup cold water
- 16 ounces (453 g) apple juice

- ⅛ cup brown sugar
- 1 cinnamon stick
- 1 cup hot water
- ¼ cup kosher salt

1. In a large pot, combine cinnamon, hot water, cold water, apple juice, brown sugar, and salt. Stir the mixture until the sugar is fully dissolved. 2. Submerge the hen in the brine, then cover the pot and refrigerate for 4 hours to let the flavors infuse. 3. Preheat the griddle to high heat, preparing it for cooking. 4. Lightly spray the griddle surface with cooking spray to prevent sticking. 5. Once the hens have finished brining, remove them from the liquid and place them on the hot griddle. Cook for about 60 minutes, or until the internal temperature reaches 160°F. 6. Once cooked, remove the hens from the griddle, slice, and serve immediately. Enjoy your flavorful dish!

# Griddled Sweet Chili Lime Chicken

**Prep time: 35 minutes | Cook time: 15 minutes | Serves 4**

- ½ cup sweet chili sauce
- ¼ cup soy sauce
- 1 teaspoon mirin
- 1 teaspoon orange juice, fresh squeezed
- 1 teaspoon orange marmalade

- 2 tablespoons lime juice
- 1 tablespoon brown sugar
- 1 clove garlic, minced
- 4 boneless, skinless chicken breasts
- Sesame seeds, for garnish

1. In a small mixing bowl, whisk together sweet chili sauce, soy sauce, mirin, orange marmalade, lime juice, orange juice, brown sugar, and minced garlic until well combined. 2. Set aside ¼ cup of the sauce for later use. 3. Toss the chicken in the remaining sauce to coat thoroughly and let it marinate for 30 minutes to absorb the flavors. 4. Preheat your griddle to medium heat. 5. Once heated, place the marinated chicken on the griddle and cook each side for about 7 minutes, or until cooked through. 6. Baste the cooked chicken with the reserved marinade, and garnish with sesame seeds before serving alongside your favorite sides. Enjoy your flavorful meal!

# Yellow Curry Chicken Wings

**Prep time: 35 minutes | Cook time: 30 minutes-1 hour | Serves 6**

- 2 pounds ( 0.9 kg) chicken wings

For the marinade:

- ½ cup Greek yogurt, plain
- 1 tablespoon mild yellow curry powder
- 1 tablespoon olive oil
- ½ teaspoon sea salt
- ½ teaspoon black pepper
- 1 teaspoon red chili flakes

1. Start by rinsing the chicken wings thoroughly and patting them dry with paper towels. 2. In a large mixing bowl, whisk together the marinade ingredients until they are well combined. 3. Add the wings to the bowl and toss them to ensure they are evenly coated in the marinade. 4. Cover the bowl with plastic wrap and chill in the refrigerator for 30 minutes to let the flavors meld. 5. For prep time, it takes about 10 minutes, and the cook time is another 10 minutes, serving 4. Preheat one side of the griddle to medium heat and the other side to medium-high heat. 6. Working in batches, place the wings on the medium heat side of the griddle and cook, turning occasionally, until the skin begins to brown, approximately 12 minutes. 7. Once browned, move the wings to the medium-high heat side of the griddle and cook for an additional 5 minutes on each side, charring them until they are cooked through. Ensure the internal temperature reaches 165°F when measured at the bone. 8. Finally, transfer the wings to a platter and serve warm for a delicious appetizer or meal. Enjoy!

# Hoisin-Glazed Grilled Turkey Wings

**Prep time: 15 minutes | Cook time: 1 hour | Serves 8**

- 2 pounds ( 0.9 kg) turkey wings
- ½ cup hoisin sauce
- 1 tablespoon honey
- 2 teaspoons soy sauce
- 2 garlic cloves (minced)
- 1 teaspoon freshly grated ginger
- 2 teaspoons sesame oil
- 1 teaspoon pepper or to taste
- 1 teaspoon salt or to taste
- ¼ cup pineapple juice
- 1 tablespoon chopped green onions
- 1 tablespoon sesame seeds
- 1 lemon (cut into wedges)

1. In a large container, combine honey, minced garlic, grated ginger, soy sauce, hoisin sauce, sesame oil, pepper, and salt. Transfer the mixture into a zip-lock bag and add the chicken wings. Seal the bag and refrigerate for 2 hours to let the flavors meld. 2. After marinating, remove the turkey wings from the marinade and set aside the marinade for later use. Allow the wings to rest for a few minutes until they reach room temperature. Preheat your griddle to 300°F, keeping the lid closed for about 15 minutes. 3. Arrange the marinated wings in a grilling basket and place the basket on the griddle. 4. Cook the wings for 1 hour, or until the internal temperature reaches 165°F. 5. While the wings are cooking, pour the reserved marinade into a saucepan over medium-high heat. Stir in pineapple juice and bring the mixture to a boil. Then, reduce the heat and let it simmer until the sauce thickens. 6. Brush the cooked wings with the thickened sauce and continue cooking for an additional 6 minutes. Once done, remove the wings from the heat. 7. Serve the wings garnished with chopped green onions, sesame seeds, and lemon wedges for added flavor and presentation. Enjoy your delicious wings!

# Jalapeno Injection Turkey

**Prep time: 15 minutes | Cook time: 4 hours 10 minutes | Serves 4**

- 15 pounds (6.8 kg) whole turkey, giblet removed
- ½ of medium red onion, peeled and minced
- 8 jalapeño peppers
- 2 tablespoons minced garlic
- 4 tablespoons garlic powder
- 6 tablespoons Italian seasoning
- 1 cup butter, softened, unsalted
- ¼ cup olive oil
- 1 cup chicken broth

1. Begin by opening the hopper of the griddle and adding dry pellets. Ensure that the ash can is properly in place, then open the ash damper. Power on the griddle and close the ash damper to prepare for cooking. 2. Set the temperature of the griddle to 200°F and allow it to preheat for about 30 minutes, or until the green light on the dial blinks, indicating that the griddle has reached the desired temperature. 3. While the griddle is heating, place a large saucepan over medium-high heat. Add a combination of oil and butter. Once the butter melts, add chopped onion, minced garlic, and diced peppers, cooking for 3 to 5 minutes until they are golden brown and fragrant. 4. Pour in the broth and stir well to combine. Let the mixture come to a boil for 5 minutes, then remove the pan from heat and strain it to extract just the liquid. 5. Generously inject the prepared liquid into the turkey to infuse it with flavor. Next, spray the outside of the turkey with butter spray and season it thoroughly with garlic and Italian seasoning for an extra layer of taste. 6. Place the seasoned turkey on the griddle, close the lid, and smoke for 30 minutes. Afterward, increase the temperature to 325°F and continue smoking the turkey for an additional 3 hours, or until the internal temperature reaches 165°F. 7. Once done, transfer the turkey to a cutting board and let it rest for about 5 minutes. After resting, carve the turkey into slices and serve. Enjoy your flavorful smoked turkey!

# Sage and Apple Smoked Turkey

**Prep time: 10 minutes | Cook time: 5 hours | Serves 6**

- 1 (10-12 pounds / 4.5 kg-5.4 kg) turkey, giblets removed
- Extra-virgin olive oil, for rubbing
- ¼ cup poultry seasoning
- 8 tablespoons (1 stick) unsalted butter, melted
- ½ cup apple juice
- 2 teaspoons dried sage
- 2 teaspoons dried thyme

1. Begin by following the manufacturer's specific startup procedure for your griddle. Preheat the griddle with the lid closed until it reaches 250°F. 2. Rub the turkey thoroughly with oil, then season it generously with poultry seasoning on both the inside and outside, making sure to get some underneath the skin for maximum flavor. 3. In a separate bowl, combine melted butter, apple juice, sage, and thyme to create a basting mixture. 4. Place the turkey in a roasting pan and set it on the griddle. Close the lid and cook for 5 to 6 hours, basting every hour with the prepared mixture, until the skin is brown and crispy. Use a meat thermometer to check that the internal temperature in the thickest part of the thigh reaches 165°F. 5. Once done, remove the turkey from the griddle and let it rest for about 15 to 20 minutes before carving to allow the juices to redistribute. Enjoy your perfectly cooked turkey!

# Hasselback Tex-Mex Stuffed Chicken

**Prep time: 15 minutes | Cook time: 30 minutes | Serves 4**

- boneless, skinless chicken breasts
- 2 tablespoons olive oil
- 2 tablespoons taco seasoning
- ½ red, yellow and green pepper, very thinly sliced
- small red onion, very thinly sliced
- ½ cup Mexican shredded cheese
- Guacamole, for serving
- Sour cream, for serving
- Salsa, for serving

1. Preheat the griddle to medium-high heat to prepare for cooking the chicken. 2. Make thin horizontal cuts across each chicken breast, similar to hasselback potatoes, ensuring not to cut all the way through. 3. Rub the chicken breasts evenly with olive oil and sprinkle taco seasoning over them for added flavor. 4. Stuff each cut with a mixture of bell peppers and red onions, then place the seasoned breasts on the hot griddle. 5. Cook the chicken for about 15 minutes, allowing it to cook through thoroughly. 6. Once cooked, remove the chicken from the griddle and top each breast with shredded cheese. 7. Tent the chicken loosely with foil and return it to the griddle for an additional 5 minutes, or until the cheese is melted and bubbly. 8. After cooking, remove the chicken from the griddle and top with guacamole, sour cream, and salsa for a delicious finishing touch. Serve alongside your favorite side dishes for a complete meal! Enjoy!

# Chicken Tacos With Avocado Crema

**Prep time: 1 hour 5 minutes | Cook time: 10 minutes | Serves 4-5**

- ½ pound (227 g) Boneless, skinless chicken breasts, sliced thin

For the chicken marinade:
- 1 serrano pepper, minced
- 2 teaspoons garlic, minced
- 1 lime, juiced
- 1 teaspoon ground cumin
- ⅓ cup olive oil
- Sea salt, to taste
- Black pepper, to taste

For the avocado crema:
- 1 cup sour cream
- 2 teaspoons lime juice
- 1 teaspoon lime zest
- 1 serrano pepper, diced and seeded
- 1 clove garlic, minced
- 1 large hass avocado

For the garnish:
- ½ cup queso fresco, crumbled
- 2 teaspoons cilantro, chopped
- 1 lime sliced into wedges
- 10 corn tortillas

1. In a sealable plastic bag, combine all the ingredients for the chicken marinade. Add the chicken pieces and toss to coat thoroughly. 2. Let the chicken marinate in the refrigerator for 1 hour to enhance the flavors. 3. While the chicken marinates, prepare the avocado crema by adding all its ingredients to a food processor or blender. Pulse until the mixture is smooth and creamy. 4. Cover the crema and refrigerate until you're ready to assemble the tacos. 5. Preheat the griddle to medium heat. Once hot, place the marinated chicken on the griddle and cook for about 5 minutes per side, rotating and turning as needed for even cooking. 6. After cooking, remove the chicken from the griddle and tent it loosely with aluminum foil. Allow it to rest for 5 minutes before slicing. 7. Serve the sliced chicken with warm tortillas, a generous dollop of avocado crema, crumbled queso fresco, fresh cilantro, and lime wedges for squeezing. 8. For meal prep: Prepare in 10 minutes, cook for another 10 minutes, and this recipe serves 4. Simply divide the chicken into individual portion containers along with the garnishes, and wrap tortillas in parchment paper to warm in the microwave when ready to serve. Enjoy your delicious tacos!

# Grilled Thai Chili Glazed Chicken Quarters

- chicken leg quarters, lightly coated with olive oil
- cup and 1 teaspoon water
- ¾ cup rice vinegar
- ½ cup white sugar
- 1 tablespoon freshly chopped cilantro
- 1 tablespoon freshly minced ginger root

- 2 teaspoons.freshly minced garlic
- 2 tablespoons crushed red pepper flakes
- 2 tablespoons ketchup
- 2 tablespoons cornstarch
- 2 tablespoons fresh basil chiffonade ("chiffonade" is fancy for "thinly sliced")

1. In a medium-sized saucepan, combine 1 cup of water and vinegar, bringing the mixture to a boil over high heat. 2. Once boiling, stir in sugar, chopped cilantro, ginger, minced garlic, red pepper flakes, and ketchup. Reduce the heat and let it simmer for 5 minutes to meld the flavors. 3. In a small mixing bowl, combine 1 teaspoon of warm water with 2 tablespoons of cornstarch, mixing well with a fork until the mixture resembles white school glue. 4. Gradually whisk the cornstarch mixture into the simmering sauce, stirring continuously until the sauce thickens. Set aside once thickened. 5. Preheat the griddle to high heat. When hot, place the chicken quarters skin side down on the griddle and cook for 8 minutes, allowing the skin to crisp up. 6. When the internal temperature of the chicken reaches 155°F, glaze the chicken with the prepared sauce and continue cooking until it reaches an internal temperature of 165°F. 7. Once cooked, plate the chicken quarters, garnish with fresh basil, and serve immediately. Enjoy your flavorful dish!

# Honey-Glazed Smoked Chicken

- 1 (4 pounds / 1.81 kg) of chicken with the giblets thoroughly removed and patted dry
- 1½ lemon

- 1 tablespoon of honey
- 4 tablespoons of unsalted butter
- 4 tablespoon of chicken seasoning

1. Fire up your griddle and set the temperature to 225°F to prepare for smoking the chicken. 2. In a small saucepan, melt the butter together with honey over low heat, stirring until combined. 3. Once melted, squeeze in the juice of ½ lemon and then remove the mixture from the heat source. 4. Place the chicken on the griddle, skin side down, and smoke it until the skin turns light brown and starts to release from the grate. 5. Carefully turn the chicken over and brush it generously with the honey butter mixture. 6. Continue to smoke the chicken, tasting it every 45 minutes, until the thickest part of the meat reaches an internal temperature of 160°F. 7. Once cooked, remove the chicken from the griddle and let it rest for 5 minutes before serving. Garnish with the leftover sliced lemon for an extra burst of flavor and enjoy your delicious dish!

# Grilled Chicken Satay with Creamy Almond Butter Sauce

Prep time: 2 hours 20 minutes | Cook time: 8 minutes | Serves 4

- 1 pound (454 g) boneless, skinless chicken thighs, cut into thin strips

For the marinade:

- ½ cup canned light coconut milk
- ½ lime, juiced
- 1 tablespoon honey
- 2 teaspoons soy sauce
- 1½ teaspoons fish sauce

For the almond butter sauce:

- ¼ cup almond butter
- ¼ cup water
- 2 tablespoons canned, light coconut milk
- 1 tablespoon honey
- ½ lime, juiced

- Olive oil, for brushing

- ½ teaspoon red chili flakes
- 2 teaspoons ginger, grated
- 1 clove of garlic, grated
- ½ teaspoon curry powder
- ¼ teaspoon ground coriander

- 1 teaspoon fish sauce
- 1 teaspoon fresh grated ginger
- ½ teaspoon low sodium soy sauce
- ½ teaspoon Sriracha

1. In a medium mixing bowl, whisk together all the ingredients for the marinade until well combined. 2. Add the chicken to the mixing bowl and toss to ensure each piece is thoroughly coated in the marinade. 3. Cover the bowl and refrigerate for 2 hours, or ideally overnight, to allow the flavors to penetrate the chicken. 4. Preheat the griddle to medium-high heat and brush the surface with olive oil to prevent sticking. 5. Thread the marinated chicken strips onto metal skewers, ensuring they are evenly spaced. 6. Place the chicken skewers on the prepared griddle and cook for 3 minutes. Rotate the skewers and cook for an additional 4 minutes, or until the chicken is fully cooked through. 7. While the chicken is cooking, whisk together all the ingredients for the almond butter sauce in a small saucepan. 8. Bring the sauce to a boil over medium heat, then reduce to medium-low and let it simmer for 1 to 2 minutes, or until it thickens to your desired consistency. 9. Serve the chicken satay warm, drizzled with the almond butter sauce, and enjoy your flavorful dish!

# Cured Turkey Drumstick

Prep time: 20 minutes | Cook time: 2.5 to 3 hours | Serves 3

- 3 fresh or thawed frozen turkey drumsticks
- 3 tablespoons extra virgin olive oil
- Brine component
- 4 cups of filtered water
- ¼ cup kosher salt

- ¼ cup brown sugar
- 1 teaspoon garlic powder
- poultry seasoning 1 teaspoon
- ½ teaspoon red pepper flakes
- 1 teaspoon pink hardened salt

1. In a 1-gallon sealable bag, combine the ingredients for the saltwater brine. Add the turkey drumstick to the brine and refrigerate for 12 hours. After the brining period, remove the drumstick from the saline solution, rinse it thoroughly with cold water, and pat it dry with a paper towel. 2. To enhance the skin's texture, air dry the drumstick in the refrigerator without covering it for 2 hours. Afterward, remove the drumstick from the refrigerator and rub a tablespoon of extra virgin olive oil both under and over the skin of each drumstick. 3. Preheat the griddle for indirect cooking, setting it to 250°F. 4. Once the griddle is hot, place the drumstick on the griddle and smoke it at 250°F for 2 hours. After this initial cooking time, increase the griddle temperature to 325°F. 5. Continue cooking the turkey drumstick at 325°F until the internal temperature in the thickest part reaches 180°F, as measured by an instant-read digital thermometer. 6. Once done, remove the smoked turkey drumstick and place it under a loose foil tent for about 15 minutes before serving. Enjoy your delicious smoked turkey drumstick!

# Chapter

# 6

# Vegetables and Sides

# Chapter 6 Vegetables and Sides

## Beer-Smoked Garlic-Rubbed Cabbage

**Prep time: 40 minutes | Cook time: 3 hours | Serves 10**

- 3 pounds (1.36 kg) whole cabbages
- 3 tablespoons olive oil
- 2 teaspoons garlic powder
- ¼ teaspoon salt
- ¼ teaspoon chili powder
- ½ teaspoon ground cinnamon
- 1 can beer

1. In a bowl, combine garlic powder, salt, chili powder, and ground cinnamon to create a spice mix. 2. Drizzle olive oil over the spices and mix well until fully combined. 3. Rub the spice mixture generously over the cabbage, making sure to get it in between the leaves for maximum flavor. 4. Preheat the griddle for indirect heat and adjust the temperature to 275°F (135°C). 5. Place the seasoned cabbage on a sheet of aluminum foil, wrapping it tightly while leaving the top open for ventilation. 6. Pour beer over the cabbage, allowing it to soak in, then place the wrapped cabbage on the griddle. Smoke the cabbage for about 3 hours, or until it becomes tender. 7. Once finished, carefully remove the smoked cabbage from the griddle and unwrap it. 8. Cut the smoked cabbage into wedges and arrange them on a serving platter. 9. Enjoy your delicious smoked cabbage!

## Naan-Style Flatbread

**Prep time: 8 minutes | Cook time: 15 minutes | Serves 8**

- 1 cup warm water
- 1 teaspoon sugar
- 1 tablespoon instant dry yeast
- 3 cups all-purpose flour
- ½ cup plain yogurt
- 1 tablespoon olive oil
- 1 teaspoon salt
- cooking oil, as needed

1. In a large bowl, combine warm water, sugar, and yeast, stirring gently. Let the mixture sit for about 10 minutes to allow the yeast to activate and become frothy. 2. Once the yeast is activated, add the remaining ingredients (except for the cooking oil) to the bowl. Mix until the dough is smooth and well combined. 3. Cover the bowl with a cloth and let the dough rest and rise for 1 hour in a warm place. After rising, turn the dough out onto a floured surface. 4. Preheat the griddle to medium heat. Divide the rested dough into eight equal balls. Roll each ball out into a flat round, about ¼ to ⅛ inch thick. 5. Lightly coat the griddle with cooking oil, then place the rolled-out dough rounds onto the hot griddle. Cook for 1 to 2 minutes on each side until they are golden and cooked through. Enjoy your delicious homemade flatbreads!

## Green Beans with Bacon

**Prep time: 10 minutes | Cook time: 20 minutes | Serves 6**

- 4 strips of bacon, chopped
- 1½ pounds (680 g) green beans, ends trimmed
- 1 teaspoon minced garlic
- 1 teaspoon salt
- 4 tablespoons olive oil

1. Turn on the griddle and set it to 450°F, allowing it to preheat for at least 15 minutes. 2. While it's heating, take a sheet tray and combine all the ingredients; toss them together until well mixed. 3. Once the griddle is hot, lift the lid, place the prepared sheet tray on the griddle grate, close the lid, and smoke for 20 minutes until the green beans are lightly browned and fully cooked. 4. Transfer the green beans to a serving dish and enjoy right away.

## Griddle Zucchini Squash Spears

**Prep time: 5 minutes | Cook time: 10 minutes | Serves 4 to 6**

- 4 medium zucchinis
- 2 tablespoons olive oil
- 1 tablespoon cherry vinegar
- 2 springs thyme, leaves pulled
- Salt and pepper, to taste

1. Clean the zucchini and trim both ends, then cut each zucchini in half and each half into thirds. 2. Preheat the griddle to 350°F, closing the lid for about 15 minutes. 3. Grill the zucchini for 3-4 minutes per side, until tender with nice griddle marks. 4. Remove from the griddle and garnish with extra thyme leaves if desired. Enjoy!

# Butter-Basted Cauliflower with Parmesan

- 1 medium head of cauliflower
- 1 teaspoon minced garlic
- 1 teaspoon salt
- ½ teaspoon ground black pepper
- ¼ cup olive oil
- ½ cup melted butter, unsalted
- ½ tablespoon chopped parsley
- ¼ cup shredded parmesan cheese

1. Turn on the griddle, set the temperature to 450°F, and allow it to preheat for at least 15 minutes. 2. While the griddle is heating, brush the cauliflower head with oil, then season it with salt and black pepper. Place the seasoned cauliflower in a griddle pan. 3. Once the griddle has preheated, open the lid and place the prepared griddle pan on the griddle grate. Close the lid and smoke the cauliflower for 45 minutes, or until it is golden brown and tender in the center. 4. In the meantime, take a small bowl and add melted butter. Stir in minced garlic, chopped parsley, and cheese until well combined. 5. During the last 20 minutes of cooking, baste the cauliflower frequently with the cheese mixture. Once the cooking time is complete, remove the pan from the heat and garnish the cauliflower with additional parsley. 6. Cut the smoked cauliflower into slices and serve immediately. Enjoy your flavorful dish!

# Cinnamon-Spiced Smoked Acorn Squash

- 2 pounds ( 0.9 kg) acorn squash
- 3 tablespoons butter
- ¼ cup brown sugar
- ¼ teaspoon salt
- ¼ teaspoon ground cinnamon
- ¼ teaspoon ground ginger
- ¼ teaspoon ground nutmeg

1. In a bowl, combine brown sugar, salt, ground cinnamon, ground ginger, and ground nutmeg. Mix well and set aside for later use. 2. Cut the acorn squash in half and place the halves in a disposable aluminum pan with the cut sides facing up. 3. Brush melted butter over the cut sides of the acorn squash, then generously sprinkle the brown sugar mixture on top. Set aside for now. 4. Preheat the griddle for indirect heat, adjusting the temperature to 225°F (107°C). 5. Once the griddle is ready, place the prepared acorn squash on it and smoke for about 2 hours, or until the squash is tender. 6. After smoking, carefully remove the acorn squash from the griddle and transfer it to a serving dish. 7. Serve warm and enjoy your deliciously smoked acorn squash!

# Grilled Asian-Style Broccoli

- 4 tablespoons soy sauce
- 4 tablespoons balsamic vinegar
- 2 tablespoons canola oil
- 2 teaspoons maple syrup
- 2 heads broccoli, trimmed into florets
- Red pepper flakes, for garnish
- Sesame seeds, for garnish

1. Preheat the griddle to medium-high heat to get it ready for cooking. 2. While the griddle is heating, combine soy sauce, balsamic vinegar, oil, and maple syrup in a large bowl. Whisk the ingredients together until well blended. Add the broccoli florets to the bowl and toss to ensure they are evenly coated with the marinade. 3. Once the griddle is hot, place the marinated broccoli on it and grill for 8 to 10 minutes, turning occasionally, until the broccoli is charred on all sides. 4. When cooking is complete, transfer the grilled broccoli to a large serving platter. Garnish with red pepper flakes and sesame seeds for added flavor and presentation. Serve immediately and enjoy your delicious grilled broccoli!

# Smoky Parmesan Roasted Cauliflower

- 1 cauliflower head, cut into florets
- 1 tablespoon oil
- 1 cup parmesan, grated
- 2 garlic cloves, crushed
- ½ teaspoon pepper
- ½ teaspoon salt
- ¼ teaspoon paprika

1. Preheat your griddle to 180°F to prepare for smoking. 2. Once heated, transfer the cauliflower florets to the griddle and smoke them for 1 hour, allowing the flavors to develop. 3. In a separate bowl, combine all the ingredients except for the cheese, mixing well. 4. After the smoking time is complete, remove the florets from the griddle. 5. Increase the griddle temperature to 450°F. Brush the florets with the mixture you prepared earlier, then transfer them back to the griddle. 6. Smoke the florets for an additional 10 minutes at this higher temperature. 7. Sprinkle the cheese on top of the florets and close the lid, allowing them to sit until the cheese melts. 8. Once melted, serve the cheesy smoked cauliflower florets and enjoy your delicious creation!

# Griddle Potato Salad

Prep time: 15 minutes | Cook time: 10 minutes | Serves 8

- 1½ pounds (680 g) fingerling potatoes, halved lengthwise
- 1 small jalapeno, sliced
- 10 scallions
- 2 teaspoons salt
- 2 tablespoons rice vinegar
- 2 teaspoons lemon juice
- ⅔ cup olive oil, divided

1. Turn on the griddle and set the temperature to 450°F, allowing it to preheat for at least 5 minutes. 2. While the griddle is heating, prepare the scallions by brushing them lightly with oil. 3. Once the griddle is preheated, open the lid, place the scallions on the griddle grate, and close the lid to smoke them for about 3 minutes, or until they are lightly charred. 4. After smoking, transfer the scallions to a cutting board, let them cool for 5 minutes, then slice them and set aside for later use. 5. Next, brush the potatoes with oil and season with salt and black pepper. Place the seasoned potatoes on the griddle grate, close the lid, and smoke for 5 minutes, or until they are thoroughly cooked. 6. In a large bowl, combine the remaining oil, salt, lemon juice, and vinegar, stirring until well mixed. 7. Add the grilled scallions and potatoes to the bowl, tossing everything together until evenly combined. Taste and adjust the seasoning as needed before serving. Enjoy your delicious smoked scallions and potatoes!

# Baked Green Bean Casserole

Prep time: 10 minutes | Cook time: 50 minutes | Serves 10 to 12

- 3 pounds (1.36 kg) trimmed green beans
- Kosher salt
- 2 tablespoons olive oil
- 2 tablespoons unsalted butter
- ½ pound (227 g) shitake or king trumpet mushrooms, sliced
- ¼ cup minced shallot
- ¼ cup rice flour
- 2 cups chicken stock
- ½ cup sherry cooking wine
- 1 cup heavy cream
- 1 cup grated parmigiana Reggiano
- 1 cup slivered almonds, for topping
- 4 cups canola or vegetable oil
- 8 whole, peeled shallots
- ½ cup rice flour
- 1 teaspoon kosher salt

1. When you're ready to start cooking, set the temperature of the griddle to high and preheat it with the lid closed for about 15 minutes. 2. In the meantime, fill a large stockpot two-thirds full of water and bring it to a boil over high heat. Prepare a large bowl of ice water for an ice bath. Once the water is boiling, add 1 tablespoon of salt. 3. When the water returns to a rolling boil, add half of the green beans. Cook until they are al dente, approximately 2 minutes. Use a strainer to remove the beans and immediately transfer them to the ice bath to cool down. 4. After cooling, remove the green beans from the ice water and place them on paper towels to dry. Repeat this process with the remaining green beans. Alternatively, you can place them on a clean dish towel and roll it up to remove excess water. 5. To prepare the sauce, melt butter and olive oil in a small saucepan over medium heat. Add shallots and mushrooms, along with a generous pinch of salt, and cook while stirring for about 5 minutes, until the mushrooms become soft. 6. Sprinkle rice flour over the mushroom mixture and stir well to coat. Cook for about 2 minutes to eliminate the raw flour taste, then add sherry. Stir and reduce the mixture, then gradually stir in the stock, allowing it to thicken and ensuring there are no lumps, which should take about 3 minutes. 7. Stir in the cream and Parmigiano-Reggiano cheese, tasting and adjusting the seasoning with salt and pepper as necessary. 8. Combine the blanched green beans with the prepared sauce, mixing well to coat. 9. While the green beans are warming on the griddle, prepare the fried shallots. In a deep saucepan or Dutch oven, heat oil to 350°F. 10. In a shallow bowl, mix rice flour and salt with a fork. 11. Once the casserole is ready, garnish with the fried shallots. Enjoy your delicious green bean casserole!

# Grilled Lemon–Garlic Artichokes

Prep time: 10 minutes | Cook time: 15 minutes | Serves 4

- Juice of ½ lemon
- ½ cup canola oil
- 3 garlic cloves, chopped - Sea salt
- Freshly ground black pepper
- 2 large artichokes, trimmed and halved

1. Begin by heating your griddle to a medium-high temperature, allowing it to warm up thoroughly. 2. While the griddle is preheating, prepare the marinade in a medium bowl by mixing together fresh lemon juice, olive oil, and minced garlic. Season this mixture with salt and pepper to taste. 3. Brush the cut sides of the artichoke halves generously with the lemon-garlic blend, ensuring they're well-coated. 4. Place the artichokes on the griddle with the cut side facing down, pressing gently to enhance those beautiful grill marks. Grill for 8 to 10 minutes, occasionally basting with the marinade to keep them flavorful, until they are nicely blistered and charred all over. 5. Once done, remove the artichokes from the griddle and let them cool slightly before serving. Enjoy your deliciously grilled artichokes as a flavorful side or appetizer!

# Caramelized Smoked Onions with Molasses Glaze

Prep time: 30 minutes | Cook time: 1hour | Serves 10

- 2½ pounds (1.1 kg) onions
- ½ cup salted butter
- 3 tablespoons brown sugar
- 1 tablespoon molasses
- 2 tablespoons apple cider vinegar
- 1 tablespoon worcestershire sauce
- 2 teaspoons dry mustard
- 1 teaspoon smoked paprika
- 1 teaspoon onion powder

1. Peel and slice the onions, placing them in a disposable aluminum pan. 2. In a bowl, mix brown sugar, molasses, apple cider vinegar, Worcestershire sauce, dry mustard, smoked paprika, and onion powder; sprinkle this mixture over the onions and shake to coat. 3. Dot the top with butter and set aside. 4. Preheat the griddle for indirect heat at 225°F (107°C). 5. Place the aluminum pan in the griddle and smoke for 1.5 hours, until caramelized. 6. Remove the smoked onions, stir gently, and transfer to a serving dish. 7. Serve and enjoy!

# Fried Rice

Prep time: 8 minutes | Cook time: 15 minutes | Serves 4

- ½ cup soy sauce
- ½ cup water
- ½ cup oyster sauce
- 2 tablespoons sesame oil
- 1 tablespoon sriracha (optional)
- ½ cup finely diced carrots
- ½ cup diced sweet onions
- 4 cloves garlic, minced
- ½ cup frozen peas
- 4 cups cooked rice, cooled
- ½ cup finely sliced scallions, divided
- cooking oil, as needed

1. In a medium bowl, whisk together soy sauce, water, oyster sauce, sesame oil, and sriracha (if using). Set the sauce aside for later. 2. Preheat the griddle to medium-high heat and add a drizzle of cooking oil to the surface. When the oil starts to shimmer, add sliced carrots, diced onions, and minced garlic. Cook while stirring frequently for about 5 minutes, until the onions become translucent. Add peas to the mixture and push the vegetables to one side of the griddle. 3. In the open space on the griddle, add a bit more cooking oil and spread the cooked rice in an even layer. Heat the rice for 3 to 4 minutes, allowing it to brown slightly. 4. Gather the rice into a large, tall mound, then add about half of the fried rice sauce and half of the chopped scallions, along with the cooked vegetables. Using a large spatula, mix everything together thoroughly, then flatten the rice back into a single layer on the griddle. This allows any liquids to evaporate and be absorbed by the rice. As the rice soaks up the sauce, it will darken in color. Continue adding the fried rice sauce, flipping and mixing the rice until it is evenly coated. 5. Once the rice is well mixed and heated through, transfer it to a serving platter and garnish with the remaining scallions. Enjoy your delicious fried rice!

# Griddled Zucchini

Prep time: 5 minutes | Cook time: 10 minutes | Serves 6

- 4 medium zucchini
- 2 tablespoons olive oil
- 1 tablespoon sherry vinegar
- 2 sprigs of thyme, leaves chopped
- ½ teaspoon salt
- ⅓ teaspoon ground black pepper

1. Start by turning on your griddle and setting it to 350 degrees F, allowing it to preheat for at least 5 minutes. While it's warming up, prepare the zucchini by trimming the ends, cutting each zucchini in half, and then into thirds, placing the pieces in a plastic bag. 2. Add the remaining ingredients to the bag, seal it tightly, and shake vigorously to ensure all the zucchini is well-coated. 3. Once the griddle is ready, open the lid and arrange the zucchini on the griddle grate. Close the lid and smoke them for 4 minutes on each side. 4. After cooking, transfer the zucchini to a serving dish, garnish with additional thyme, and enjoy your deliciously smoky treat!

# Sesame Seared Green Beans

Prep time: 10 minutes | Cook time: 10 minutes | Serves 4

- 1½ pounds (680 g) green beans, trimmed
- 1½ tablespoons rice vinegar
- 3 tablespoons soy sauce
- 1½ tablespoons sesame oil
- 2 tablespoons sesame seeds, toasted
- 1½ tablespoons brown sugar
- ¼ teaspoon black pepper

1. Begin by cooking the green beans in a pot of boiling water for 3 minutes, then drain them well. 2. Transfer the green beans to a bowl of chilled ice water to stop the cooking process, then drain again and pat them dry. 3. Preheat your griddle to high heat. 4. Once hot, add a drizzle of oil to the griddle. 5. Toss in the green beans and stir-fry for 2 minutes. 6. Next, add soy sauce, brown sugar, vinegar, and pepper, continuing to stir-fry for an additional 2 minutes. 7. Finally, sprinkle in sesame seeds and toss everything together to coat. Serve and enjoy your vibrant dish!

# Griddled Roasted Tomatoes with Spicy Pepper Sauce

**Prep time: 20 minutes | Cook time: 90 minutes | Serves 4 to 6**

- 2 pounds ( 0.9 kg) roman fresh tomatoes
- 3 tablespoons parsley, chopped
- 2 tablespoons garlic, chopped
- Black pepper, to taste
- ½ cup olive oil
- Hot pepper, to taste
- 1 pound (454 g) spaghetti or other pasta

1. When you're ready to cook, set the temperature to 400°F and preheat with the lid closed for 15 minutes. 2. Rinse the tomatoes and slice them in half lengthwise, then place them in a baking dish with the cut sides facing up. 3. Sprinkle with chopped parsley and minced garlic, season with salt and black pepper, and drizzle ¼ cup of olive oil over the top. 4. Place the baking dish on the preheated griddle and bake for 1½ hours; the tomatoes will shrink and the skins will begin to blacken. 5. Once done, remove the tomatoes from the baking dish and transfer them to a food processor, retaining the cooked oil, and puree until smooth. 6. Cook the pasta in boiling salted water until tender, then drain and immediately toss it with the pureed tomatoes. 7. Add the remaining ¼ cup of raw olive oil and crumbled hot red pepper to taste; toss well and serve. Enjoy your meal!

# Home Fries With Veggies

**Prep time: 10 minutes | Cook time: 25 minutes | Serves 4**

- 3 baked russet potatoes, cut to 1-inch cubes
- ½ cup cooked or frozen broccoli florets
- ½ cup cooked or frozen diced onion
- 3 cloves garlic, minced
- 1 tablespoon garlic salt
- 1 tablespoon smoked paprika
- 1 teaspoon pepper
- ½ cup corn (optional)
- ½ cup cooked black beans (optional)
- ½ cup diced ham (optional)
- ½ cup crumbled cooked sausage (optional)
- ½ cup diced bacon (optional)
- cooking oil, as needed

1. Start by heating the griddle to medium-high. Pour a generous amount of cooking oil onto the surface, and once it begins to shimmer, add the diced potatoes in a single layer. Depending on your cutting technique, each potato piece will have three or four flat sides, so let each side cook for about 3 to 5 minutes, adding more oil as necessary. 2. While the potatoes are sizzling, sauté the broccoli, onion, and garlic on the griddle for 4 to 5 minutes,

stirring occasionally until they become lightly browned. 3. Once the potatoes are golden and crispy on the outside while remaining creamy on the inside (around 10 to 12 minutes), mix in the sautéed vegetables along with garlic salt, smoked paprika, and pepper. Cook for an additional 2 to 3 minutes, adding any optional ingredients if you wish. Serve while hot for the best flavor!

# Blistered Green Beans

**Prep time: 5 minutes | Cook time: 10 minutes | Serves 4**

- 1 pound (454 g) haricots verts or green beans, trimmed
- 2 tablespoons vegetable oil
- Juice of 1 lemon
- Pinch red pepper flakes
- Flaky sea salt
- Freshly ground black pepper

1. Begin by setting your griddle to medium-high heat. While it's heating up, take a medium bowl and coat the green beans thoroughly with oil, ensuring they are evenly covered. 2. Once the griddle is ready, arrange the green beans on the grill and cook them for 8 to 10 minutes, turning them frequently to achieve a nice blister on all sides. When they're perfectly cooked, transfer the green beans to a generous serving platter. 3. Drizzle fresh lemon juice over the top, sprinkle with red pepper flakes for a kick, and season with sea salt and black pepper to taste. Enjoy this vibrant and flavorful dish!

# Maple-Glazed Smoked Brussels Sprouts

**Prep time: 10 minutes | Cook time: 40 minutes | Serves 10**

- 2 pounds ( 0.9 kg) brussels sprouts
- 3 tablespoons maple syrup
- 2 tablespoons olive oil
- ¼ teaspoon salt
- ¼ teaspoon pepper
- ¼ teaspoon smoked paprika

1. In a bowl, mix together maple syrup, olive oil, salt, pepper, and smoked paprika until well combined. 2. Drizzle this flavorful mixture over the Brussels sprouts, then toss to ensure they are thoroughly coated. Spread the seasoned Brussels sprouts into a disposable aluminum pan for cooking. 3. Preheat the griddle for indirect heat, setting it to 400°F (204°C). 4. Place the coated Brussels sprouts on the griddle and smoke them for 30 minutes, or until they become beautifully browned and tender. 5. Once they are finished smoking, carefully remove the Brussels sprouts from the griddle and transfer them to a serving dish. 6. Serve immediately and savor every bite!

# Griddle Fingerling Potato Salad

- 1½ pounds (680 g) Fingerling potatoes cut in half lengthwise
- 10 scallions
- ⅔ cup Evo (extra virgin olive oil), divided use
- 2 tablespoons rice vinegar

- 2 teaspoons lemon juice
- 1 small jalapeno, sliced
- 2 teaspoons kosher salt

1. Preheat your griddle to high for 15 minutes with the lid closed. Brush the scallions with oil and place them on the griddle, cooking until lightly charred, about 2-3 minutes. Remove, let cool, then slice and set aside. 2. Brush the fingerling potatoes with oil (reserve ⅓ cup for later) and season with salt and pepper. Place them cut side down on the griddle and cook until tender, about 4-5 minutes. 3. In a bowl, whisk together the remaining olive oil, rice vinegar, salt, and lemon juice. Add the scallions, potatoes, and sliced jalapeño, mixing well. Adjust seasoning to taste and serve. Enjoy your flavorful dish!

# Lemon-Sesame Smoked Asparagus

- 2 pounds ( 0.9 kg) asparagus
- 2 tablespoons sesame oil
- 2 tablespoons lemon juice
- ¼ teaspoon grated lemon zest

- 1 teaspoon garlic powder
- ½ teaspoon salt
- ¼ teaspoon pepper

1. In a bowl, mix together grated lemon zest, garlic powder, salt, and pepper. Drizzle in lemon juice and sesame oil, then stir to combine. 2. Prepare the asparagus by trimming the ends and rubbing them with the spice mixture. 3. Wrap the seasoned asparagus tightly in aluminum foil and set aside. 4. Preheat the griddle for indirect heat at 225°F (107°C). 5. Place the foil-wrapped asparagus on the griddle and smoke for about an hour, until tender. 6. Carefully remove the asparagus from the griddle and transfer to a serving dish. 7. Enjoy your delicious smoked asparagus!

# Stir Fry Mushrooms

- 10 ounces (283 g) mushrooms, sliced
- ¼ cup olive oil
- 1 tablespoon garlic, minced

- ¼ teaspoon dried thyme
- Pepper - Salt

1. Start by heating your griddle to a high setting, making sure it's adequately hot. 2. Add 2 tablespoons of oil and let it spread and shimmer. 3. Toss in the mushrooms with minced garlic, fresh thyme, and a dash of salt and pepper. Cook until the mushrooms are perfectly tender and have a lovely golden color. 4. For added flavor, drizzle the leftover oil over the sautéed mixture before serving. Enjoy the warm, rich taste!

# Charred Garlic Sugar Snap Peas

Prep time: 15 minutes | Cook time: 10 minutes | Serves 4

- 2 pounds (0.9 kg) sugar snap peas, ends trimmed
- ½ teaspoon garlic powder
- 1 teaspoon salt
- ⅔ teaspoon ground black pepper
- 2 tablespoons olive oil

1. Preheat the griddle by turning it on or setting it to 450°F, allowing at least 15 minutes for it to reach temperature. 2. In a medium bowl, combine the peas with garlic powder and oil, then season generously with salt and black pepper; mix thoroughly and spread evenly on a sheet pan. 3. Once the griddle is hot, lift the lid, place the prepared sheet pan on the griddle grate, close the lid, and smoke for about 10 minutes until they develop a nice char. 4. Enjoy immediately for the best flavor.

# Bacon-Wrapped Smoked Jalapeño Poppers

Prep time: 15 minutes | Cook time: 60 minutes | Serves 4 to 6

- 12 medium jalapeños
- 6 slices bacon, cut in half
- 8 ounces (227 g) cream cheese, softened
- 1 cup cheese, grated
- 2 tablespoons pork & poultry rub

1. When you're ready to cook, set the temperature to 180°F and preheat with the lid closed for 15 minutes. 2. Halve the jalapeños lengthwise and carefully remove the seeds and ribs using a small spoon or paring knife. 3. In a bowl, combine softened cream cheese with the Pork & Poultry rub and grated cheese until well mixed. 4. Spoon the mixture into each jalapeño half, then wrap them with bacon and secure with a toothpick. 5. Arrange the jalapeños on a rimmed baking sheet, place them on the griddle, and smoke for 30 minutes. 6. Raise the griddle temperature to 375°F and cook for an additional 30 minutes or until the bacon reaches your preferred crispness. Serve warm and enjoy!

# Sautéed Vegetables

Prep time: 10 minutes | Cook time: 5 minutes | Serves 4

2 medium zucchini, cut into matchsticks
- 2 tablespoons coconut oil
- 2 teaspoons garlic, minced
- 1 tablespoon honey
- 3 tablespoons soy sauce
- 1 teaspoon sesame seeds
- 2 cups carrots, cut into matchsticks
- 2 cups snow peas

1. In a small bowl, combine soy sauce, minced garlic, and honey; set this mixture aside. 2. Preheat the griddle to high heat. 3. Once hot, drizzle oil over the griddle surface. 4. Add the carrots, snow peas, and zucchini, sautéing for 1-2 minutes until slightly tender. 5. Pour in the soy sauce mixture and stir-fry for another minute to combine the flavors. 6. Sprinkle sesame seeds on top for garnish and serve immediately.

# Chapter
## 7

# Snacks and Appetizers

# Chapter 7 Snacks and Appetizers

## Chickpea Crunchers

**Prep time: 10 minutes | Cook time: 30 minutes | Serves 2**

- 1 (16 ounces / 454 g) can chickpeas, drained
- ¼ cup olive oil
- 1 tablespoon ground cumin
- 1 tablespoon smoked
- paprika
- 1 teaspoon garlic powder
- 1 teaspoon onion powder
- 1 teaspoon kosher salt, plus more to taste

1. In a large bowl, mix together all the ingredients until well combined. 2. Transfer the mixture onto a cool griddle grill and set the heat to medium. 3. Gradually bring the mixture up to temperature, cooking while stirring frequently for up to 30 minutes, or until the garbanzo beans have lost most of their moisture and developed a crispy, crunchy texture. Taste and finish with additional salt if desired. Enjoy your flavorful dish!

## Griddled Avocado Pizza Bites with Bacon-Corn Salsa

**Prep time: 10 minutes | Cook time: 25 minutes | Serves 4**

- 2 small avocados
- 1 tablespoon lime juice
- ½ teaspoon garlic salt
- ½ teaspoon onion powder
- dash of hot sauce
- 1 (14 ounces / 397g) can pizza dough
- 4 strips bacon, diced
- 3 tablespoons olive oil
- ½ cup corn kernels

1. Start by removing the pits and stems from the avocados. Use a spoon to scoop the flesh from the skins and transfer it to a medium bowl. Mash the avocado and mix in lime juice, garlic salt, onion powder, and hot sauce. You can prepare this mixture up to a day in advance, but to prevent discoloration from exposure to air, cover it tightly with plastic wrap directly on the surface of the avocado in the refrigerator. 2. Preheat the griddle to medium-high heat. Roll out the pizza dough and cut it into approximately 12 squares, or use a round cookie cutter to create 12 disks. 3. On one side of the griddle, start cooking the diced bacon. On the other side, drizzle about 3 tablespoons of olive oil and spread it into a thin layer using a spatula or paper towel. Place the pizza dough on the oiled griddle and cook for about 90 seconds. As the second side of the dough cooks, add the corn to the bacon, allowing it to sauté in the bacon grease. 4. Flip the pizza dough frequently, approximately every 60 seconds, until it turns a golden brown and is cooked through, which should take about 6 minutes in total. 5. Once the bacon is crispy (but not burned, around 6 minutes), the corn should have developed some color from grilling. Use a paper towel to absorb the excess bacon fat from the bacon and corn salsa. 6. To assemble, spread about a tablespoon of the avocado mixture on each piece of grilled pizza dough, then top with a teaspoon of the corn and bacon salsa for a delicious finish!

## Curried Cauliflower Skewers

**Prep time: 15 minutes | Cook time: 15 minutes | Serves 6**

- 1 cut into florets large cauliflower head
- 1 cut into wedges onion
- 1 cut into squares yellow bell pepper
- 1 fresh lemon juice
- ¼ cup olive oil
- ½ teaspoon garlic powder
- ½ teaspoon ground ginger
- 3 teaspoons.curry powder
- ½ teaspoon salt

Intolerances:
- Gluten-Free
- Egg-Free
- Lactose-Free

1. In a large mixing bowl, combine oil, lemon juice, minced garlic, grated ginger, curry powder, and salt, whisking until well blended. Add the cauliflower florets and toss them until they are thoroughly coated with the marinade. 2. Preheat the griddle to medium heat. 3. Thread the marinated cauliflower florets, along with onion and bell pepper pieces, onto skewers. 4. Place the skewers on the hot griddle and cook for 6 to 7 minutes on each side, until the vegetables are tender and slightly charred. 5. Serve hot and enjoy your flavorful skewers!

# Griddled Sweet Potato Fries

**Prep time: 10 minutes | Cook time: 12 minutes | Serves 4**

- 2 pounds ( 0.9 kg) peeled and cut into ½-inch wedges sweet potatoes
- 2 tablespoons olive oil
- pepper and salt to taste

Intolerances:
- Gluten-Free Egg-Free
- Lactose-Free

1. Start by preheating the griddle to medium-high heat. 2. In a bowl, toss the sweet potatoes with oil, salt, and pepper until well coated. 3. Arrange the sweet potato wedges on the hot griddle and cook for 6 minutes over medium heat. 4. Flip the wedges and continue cooking for an additional 6 to 8 minutes, or until they are golden and tender. Serve immediately for a delicious side!

# Crab-Stuffed Portobello Mushrooms

**Prep time: 20 minutes | Cook time: 30 to 45 minutes | Serves 6**

- 6 medium-sized portobello mushrooms
- extra virgin olive oil
- ⅓ grated parmesan cheese cup
- club beat staffing:
- 8 ounces (227 g) fresh crab meat or canned or imitation crab meat
- 2 tablespoons extra virgin olive oil
- ⅓ chopped celery
- chopped red peppers
- ½ cup chopped green onion
- ½ cup italian breadcrumbs
- ½ cup mayonnaise
- 8 ounces (227 g) cream cheese at room temperature
- ½ teaspoon of garlic
- 1 tablespoon dried parsley
- grated parmesan cheese cup
- 1 teaspoon of old bay seasoning
- ¼ teaspoon of kosher salt
- ¼ teaspoon black pepper
- Intolerances:
- egg-free

1. Start by cleaning the mushroom cap with a damp paper towel, then cut off the stem and set it aside. 2. Use a spoon to carefully remove the brown gills from the underside of the mushroom cap and discard them. 3. Prepare the crab meat stuffing: if using canned crab meat, make sure to drain, rinse, and check for any remaining shell fragments. 4. In a frying pan over medium-high heat, warm the olive oil, then add the celery, peppers, and green onions, frying for about 5 minutes. Remove from heat and let cool. 5. In a large bowl, gently combine the cooled sautéed vegetables with the crab meat and any other ingredients you're using. 6. Cover the bowl and refrigerate the crab meat stuffing until you're ready to use it. 7. Fill each mushroom cap with the crab mixture, forming a mound in the center. 8. Drizzle with extra virgin olive oil and sprinkle Parmesan cheese over each stuffed mushroom cap. Arrange the stuffed mushrooms in a 10 x 15-inch baking dish. 9. Preheat the griddle for indirect heating to 375°F. 10. Place the baking dish on the griddle and bake for 30 to 45 minutes, or until the filling is hot (reaching 165°F or 74°C on an instant-read digital thermometer) and the mushrooms begin to release their juices. Enjoy your delicious stuffed mushrooms!

# Balsamic Mushroom Skewers

**Prep time: 10 minutes | Cook time: 10 minutes | Serves 4**

- 2 pounds ( 0.9 kg) sliced ¼-inch thick mushrooms
- ½ teaspoon chopped thyme
- 3 chopped garlic cloves
- 1 tablespoon soy sauce
- 2 tablespoons balsamic vinegar
- pepper and salt to taste

Intolerances:
- Gluten-Free
- Egg-Free
- Lactose-Free

1. Combine the mushrooms with the remaining ingredients in a mixing bowl, cover it, and let it chill in the refrigerator for 30 minutes to allow the flavors to meld. 2. After marinating, thread the mushrooms onto skewers. 3. Preheat the griddle to medium-high heat. Once hot, place the mushroom skewers on the griddle and cook for 2 to 3 minutes on each side until they are nicely charred. 4. Serve the skewers hot and enjoy!

# Southwest Chicken Drumsticks

**Prep time: 10 minutes | Cook time: 30 minutes | Serves 8**

- 2 pounds ( 0.9 kg) chicken legs
- 2 tablespoons taco
- seasoning
- 2 tablespoons olive oil

Intolerances:
- Gluten-Free
- Egg-Free
- Lactose-Free

1. Begin by preheating the griddle to medium-high heat and ensure the grates are well oiled. 2. Coat the chicken legs with oil, then generously rub them with taco seasoning for added flavor. 3. Once the griddle is hot, place the seasoned chicken legs on it and cook for a total of 30 minutes. 4. Turn the chicken legs every 10 minutes to ensure even cooking and a nice char. 5. Once cooked through, serve hot and enjoy!

# Quesadilla-Bun Chicken Fajita Sandwich

Prep time: 15 minutes | Cook time:25 minutes | Serves 2

For the fajita chicken marinade:
- ½ cup cooking oil
- 1 ounce (28g) tequila
- 2 tablespoons Worcestershire sauce
- 1 tablespoon hot sauce
- 4 cloves garlic, minced
- juice of 1 lemon

- juice of 1 lime
- 1 tablespoon ground cumin
- 1 tablespoon garlic powder
- 1 tablespoon onion powder
- 1 teaspoon salt
- 1 teaspoon pepper

For the fajitas:
- 1 (8-ounce / 227g) chicken breast, sliced into strips
- ½ Lemon Griddle Sauce, plus more for cooking
- 8 medium-sized flour tortillas
- 2 cups shredded cheddar-Jack cheese blend
- ½ green bell pepper, cut into strips

- ½ red bell pepper, cut into strips
- 1 medium, sweet onion cut into strips
- ¾ cup prepared salsa, divided
- salt and pepper, to taste

1. In a large bowl, combine all the ingredients for the fajita marinade. Add the sliced chicken, cover the bowl, and let it marinate in the refrigerator for 4 to 6 hours or overnight for maximum flavor. 2. Preheat the griddle to medium-high heat. Once hot, place the marinated chicken on the grill, discarding any leftover marinade. Cook the chicken strips, covered, for 10 to 12 minutes, turning occasionally, and add Lemon Griddle Sauce as needed to create steam and enhance cooking. 3. While the chicken cooks, warm four tortillas on the griddle. Once they're heated, evenly distribute the cheese between them, then top each with a second tortilla to create quesadilla buns. After 3 minutes, flip the quesadillas and allow the other side to warm and the cheese to melt for another 3 minutes. Keep them warm and set aside. 4. In a small amount of oil on the grill, sauté the peppers and onions for 3 to 5 minutes until they start to wilt. As they cook, season with salt and pepper, add about ½ cup of Lemon Griddle Sauce, and continue cooking for another 3 minutes, until the onions become translucent. 5. Once the chicken is cooked through, assemble your dish by placing a quesadilla on a plate, topping it with salsa, and adding the chicken, sautéed peppers, and onions. Finish with another quesadilla on top for a delicious layered meal!

# Parmesan Tomatoes

Prep time: 2 hours | Cook time: 20 minutes | Serves 6

- 9 halved Tomatoes
- 1 cup grated Parmesan cheese
- ½ teaspoon Ground black pepper
- ¼ teaspoon Onion powder

- 1 tablespoon Dried rosemary
- 2 tablespoons Olive oil
- 5 minced Garlic cloves
- 1 teaspoon Kosher salt

Intolerances:
- Gluten-Free

- Egg-Free

1. Preheat your griddle to medium-low heat, making sure to oil the grates well. 2. Place the tomato halves, cut side down, onto the griddle and allow them to cook for 5 to 7 minutes until nicely charred. 3. In a separate pan over medium heat, warm some olive oil, then add minced garlic, fresh rosemary, black pepper, onion powder, and salt, sautéing for 3 to 5 minutes until fragrant. 4. Remove the pan from heat and set the mixture aside. Flip each tomato half, then brush them generously with the olive oil and garlic mixture, topping them off with grated Parmesan cheese. 5. Close the griddle lid and cook for an additional 7 to 10 minutes, or until the cheese has melted beautifully. 6. Carefully remove the tomatoes from the griddle and serve them immediately for the best flavor!

# Crispy Ramen Pork and Veggie Cake

- ¼ pound (113g) ground pork
- ¼ cup soy sauce
- 2 tablespoons minced ginger
- 2 tablespoons minced garlic
- 2 tablespoons sesame oil
- 2 (6-ounce / 170g) packages cooked ramen noodles
- 2 cups chopped cabbage
- ¾ cup chopped kale
- ⅓ cup shredded carrot
- Asian Griddle Sauce , as needed
- cooking oil, as needed

1. Preheat the griddle to medium-high heat. Once it's hot, add the ground pork and use a spatula (or a spatula and scraper) to break it up into fine pieces, ensuring even cooking and a good texture. 2. After about 4 minutes, mix in the soy sauce, ginger, garlic, and sesame oil. Continue cooking for an additional 1 to 2 minutes until the liquids reduce, then slide the pork to a cooler area on the griddle. 3. Drizzle some oil over the cooking surface and let it heat until shimmering. Spread the cooked ramen noodles in a thin layer across the griddle, maximizing the surface area. Since the noodles are hydrated with water, the goal is to evaporate some of that moisture to achieve a crispy texture. Initially, the noodles will become gooey and gummy, but they'll eventually turn brown and crispy. After about 5 minutes, flip the noodles; be sure to scrape up any stuck bits from the griddle. If needed, add more oil sparingly to prevent sticking and promote browning. 4. Once the noodles are crispy, pile the cabbage, kale, carrots, and cooked pork on one half of the noodle layer. Place the remaining noodles on top to help wilt the vegetables. Spread everything out on the griddle and flip the noodles and veggies from the edges toward the center to enhance their contact with the griddle. Drizzle some Asian Griddle Sauce over the mixture for extra flavor. 5. As the sauce reduces and eventually evaporates, you'll notice the noodles and veggies start to brown and become crispy. Aim for a crunchy outer layer of the noodle cake while keeping the inner noodles slightly supple, creating a perfect balance of textures. Enjoy your delicious creation!

# Chapter

## 8

# Desserts

# Chapter 8 Desserts

## Coconut Chocolate Griddle Brownies

**Prep time: 15 minutes | Cook time: 25 minutes | Serves 6**

- 4 eggs
- 1 cup Cane Sugar
- ¾ cup of Coconut oil
- 4 ounces (113 g) chocolate, chopped
- ½ teaspoon of Sea salt
- ¼ cup cocoa powder, unsweetened
- ½ cup flour
- 4 ounces (113 g) Chocolate chips
- 1 teaspoon of Vanilla

1. Preheat the griddle to 350°F with the lid closed. 2. Prepare a 9x9 baking pan by greasing it and lining it with parchment paper for easy removal. 3. In a mixing bowl, combine salt, cocoa powder, and flour; stir well and set aside. 4. Melt coconut oil and chopped chocolate together in the microwave or using a double boiler, then allow it to cool slightly. 5. Stir in vanilla extract, eggs, and sugar, whisking until well combined. 6. Gradually add the flour mixture, then fold in the chocolate chips. Pour the brownie batter into the prepared pan. 7. Place the pan on the griddle grate and bake for 20 minutes. For drier brownies, extend the baking time by an additional 5 to 10 minutes. Once baked, let the brownies cool completely before cutting them into squares. Serve and enjoy your delicious treats!

## Bacon Chocolate Chip Cookies

**Prep time: 30 minutes | Cook time: 30 minutes | Serves 6**

- 8 slices cooked and crumbled bacon
- 2½ teaspoons apple cider vinegar
- 1 teaspoon vanilla
- 2 cups semisweet chocolate chips
- 2 room temp eggs
- 1½ teaspoons baking soda
- 1 cup granulated sugar
- ½ teaspoon salt
- 2¾ cups all-purpose flour
- 1 cup light brown sugar
- 1½ stick softened butter

1. In a bowl, mix together salt, baking soda, and flour until well combined. 2. In a separate bowl, cream together sugar and butter until fluffy. Reduce the mixer speed and add in the eggs, vinegar, and vanilla extract, mixing until incorporated. 3. On low speed, gradually add the flour mixture to the wet ingredients, followed by the bacon pieces and chocolate chips, mixing until just combined. 4. Preheat your griddle with the lid closed until it reaches 375°F. 5. Line a baking sheet with parchment paper and drop teaspoonfuls of cookie batter onto the sheet. Cook the cookies on the griddle, covered, for approximately 12 minutes or until they are golden brown. Enjoy your delicious cookies!

## Seasonal Fruit on the Griddle

**Prep time: 5 minutes | Cook time: 10 minutes | Serves 4**

- 2 plums, peaches apricots, etc.(choose seasonally)
- 3 tablespoons Sugar,
- turbinate
- ¼ cup of Honey
- Gelato, as desired

1. Preheat the griddle to 450°F with the lid closed. 2. Halve each piece of fruit and remove the pits. Brush the cut sides with honey and sprinkle with a little sugar. 3. Place the fruit on the griddle until grill marks appear, then set aside to cool slightly. 4. Serve each piece of grilled fruit with a scoop of gelato on top. Enjoy this delightful dessert!

## Smoked Cinnamon Sugar Pumpkin Seeds

**Prep time: 15 minutes | Cook time: 30 minutes | Serves 8**

- 2 tablespoons sugar
- Seeds from a pumpkin
- 1 teaspoon cinnamon
- 2 tablespoons melted butter

1. Preheat your griddle with the lid closed until it reaches a temperature of 350°F. 2. Clean the seeds thoroughly and toss them in melted butter until well coated. Then mix them with sugar and cinnamon until evenly coated. Spread the mixture out on a baking sheet. 3. Place the baking sheet on the griddle and smoke for 25 minutes, allowing the seeds to crisp up and absorb the flavors. 4. Serve warm and enjoy your deliciously sweet and smoky seeds!

# Griddled Chocolate Chip Walnut Cookies

**Prep time: 30 minutes | Cook time: 30 minutes | Serves 8**

- 1½ cups chopped walnuts
- 1 teaspoon vanilla
- 2 cups chocolate chips
- 1 teaspoon baking soda
- 2½ cups plain flour
- ½ teaspoon salt
- 1½ stick softened butter
- 2 eggs
- 1 cup brown sugar
- ½ cup sugar

1. Preheat your griddle with the lid closed until it reaches 350°F. 2. In a mixing bowl, combine baking soda, salt, and flour; whisk together until evenly mixed. 3. In a separate bowl, cream together brown sugar, granulated sugar, and butter until light and fluffy. Add vanilla extract and eggs, mixing until well combined. 4. Gradually add the flour mixture to the wet ingredients while continuing to beat the mixture. Once all the flour is incorporated, fold in the chocolate chips and walnuts using a spoon. 5. Line the griddle with aluminum foil. Drop spoonfuls of cookie dough onto the foil and bake for 17 minutes until golden and cooked through. Enjoy your delicious treats!

# White Chocolate Bread Pudding

**Prep time: 20 minutes | Cook time: 1hour | Serves 12**

- 1 loaf french bread
- 4 cups heavy cream
- 3 large eggs
- 2 cups white sugar
- 1 package white chocolate morsels
- ¼ cup melted butter
- 2 teaspoons vanilla
- 1 teaspoon ground nutmeg
- 1 teaspoon salt
- bourbon white chocolate sauce
- 1 package white chocolate morsels
- 1 cup heavy cream
- 2 tablespoons melted butter
- 2 tablespoons bourbon
- ½ teaspoon salt

1. Preheat the griddle to 350°F. 2. Tear the French bread into small pieces and place them in a large bowl. Pour 4 cups of heavy cream over the bread and let it soak for 30 minutes. 3. In a medium-sized bowl, whisk together eggs, sugar, softened butter, and vanilla extract. Add a package of white chocolate chips and mix gently. Season with nutmeg and salt. 4. Pour the egg mixture over the soaked French bread and stir until everything is well combined. 5. Transfer the mixture into a well-buttered 9x13-inch baking dish and place it on the griddle. 6. Cook for about 60 minutes or until the bread pudding has set and the top is golden brown. 7. For the sauce: In a saucepan over medium heat, melt butter. Add whiskey and cook for 3 to 4 minutes until the alcohol evaporates and the butter starts to brown. 8. Stir in heavy cream and heat until it begins to simmer. Remove from heat and gradually add white chocolate chips, stirring continuously until fully melted. Season with a pinch of salt and serve over the warm bread pudding. Enjoy this decadent dessert!

# Caramel Bananas

**Prep time: 15 minutes | Cook time: 15 minutes | Serves 4**

- ⅓ cup chopped pecans
- ½ cup sweetened condensed milk
- 4 slightly green bananas
- ½ cup brown sugar
- 2 tablespoons corn syrup
- ½ cup butter

1. Preheat your griddle with the lid closed until it reaches 350°F. 2. In a heavy saucepan, combine milk, corn syrup, butter, and brown sugar. Bring the mixture to a boil, then reduce the heat and let it simmer for five minutes, stirring frequently. 3. Place the bananas (with their peels still on) on the griddle and cook for five minutes. Flip the bananas and cook for an additional five minutes, until the peels are dark and may start to split. 4. Transfer the bananas to a serving platter. Cut off the ends of each banana and split the peel down the middle. Carefully remove the peel and drizzle caramel sauce over the bananas. Finish by sprinkling with pecans for added crunch. Enjoy your delicious caramelized bananas!

# Berry Layered Griddle Cake

**Prep time: 10 minutes | Cook time: 20 minutes | Serves 6**

- 2 pounds (0.9 kg) cake
- 3 cups of whipped cream
- ¼ cup melted butter
- 1 cup of blueberries
- 1 cup of raspberries
- 1 cup sliced strawberries

1. Begin by preheating the griddle to high heat with the lid closed. 2. Slice the cake loaf into ¾-inch thick pieces, aiming for about 10 slices per loaf. Brush both sides of each slice with melted butter. 3. Place the slices on the griddle and cook for 7 minutes on each side until they are golden brown and slightly crispy. Set aside to cool completely. 4. Once cooled, start layering your dessert by placing a slice of cake, followed by a layer of fresh berries, and then a generous dollop of cream. 5. Finish by sprinkling additional berries on top for a beautiful presentation, and serve immediately. Enjoy this delightful treat!

# Griddled S'mores Dip

- ◆ 12 ounces (340 g) semisweet chocolate chips
- ◆ ¼ cup milk
- ◆ 2 tablespoons melted salted butter
- ◆ 16 ounces (453 g) marshmallows
- ◆ Apple wedges
- ◆ Graham crackers

1. Start by preheating your griddle with the lid closed until it reaches a sizzling 450°F. 2. Place a cast iron skillet on the griddle and pour in the milk along with the melted butter. Stir the mixture for about a minute until well combined. 3. Once heated, evenly spread a layer of chocolate chips on top, followed by arranging marshmallows vertically on top of the chocolate to create a delightful covering. 4. Cover the skillet and let it smoke for 5 to 7 minutes, allowing the marshmallows to achieve a beautiful, light toasting. 5. Carefully remove the skillet from the heat and serve your delicious creation alongside crisp apple wedges and graham crackers for dipping. Enjoy this decadent treat!

# Juicy Loosey Cheeseburger

- ◆ 2 pounds (0.9 kg) ground beef
- ◆ 1 egg beaten
- ◆ 1 cup dry bread crumbs
- ◆ 3 tablespoons evaporated milk
- ◆ 2 tablespoons worcestershire sauce
- ◆ 1 tablespoons griddlea griddles all purpose rub
- ◆ 4 slices of cheddar cheese
- ◆ 4 buns

1. Begin by combining the ground hamburger, egg, evaporated milk, Worcestershire sauce, and seasoning in a bowl. Use your hands to mix everything thoroughly. Divide this mixture into 4 equal portions, then take each portion and split it in half. Shape these smaller portions into flat patties, aiming for a total of 8 evenly flattened patties that will later form 4 burgers. 2. Once you have your patties flattened, place a slice of cheese in the center of one patty and cover it with another patty. Press the edges firmly to seal, and if necessary, push the meat inward slightly to create a thicker patty. Make sure the patties are slightly larger than standard burger buns, as they will shrink during cooking. 3. Preheat your grill to 300°F. 4. Remember, since you're grilling two thin patties (one on each side), the cooking times will vary. Cook the burgers for 5 to 8 minutes on each side—closer to 5 minutes for medium-rare and up to 8 minutes if you prefer them well-done. 5. When flipping the burgers, use a toothpick to poke a hole in the center of each burger to allow steam to escape. This prevents any bursting and helps avoid a guest getting burned by hot melted cheese on their first bite. 6. Serve the burgers on nice rolls and add toppings that complement the flavors of your cheesy creations. Enjoy your delicious stuffed burgers!

# Appendix 1: Measurement Conversion Chart

## VOLUME EQUIVALENTS(DRY)

| US STANDARD | METRIC (APPROXIMATE) |
|---|---|
| 1/8 teaspoon | 0.5 mL |
| 1/4 teaspoon | 1 mL |
| 1/2 teaspoon | 2 mL |
| 3/4 teaspoon | 4 mL |
| 1 teaspoon | 5 mL |
| 1 tablespoon | 15 mL |
| 1/4 cup | 59 mL |
| 1/2 cup | 118 mL |
| 3/4 cup | 177 mL |
| 1 cup | 235 mL |
| 2 cups | 475 mL |
| 3 cups | 700 mL |
| 4 cups | 1 L |

## WEIGHT EQUIVALENTS

| US STANDARD | METRIC (APPROXIMATE) |
|---|---|
| 1 ounce | 28 g |
| 2 ounces | 57 g |
| 5 ounces | 142 g |
| 10 ounces | 284 g |
| 15 ounces | 425 g |
| 16 ounces (1 pound) | 455 g |
| 1.5 pounds | 680 g |
| 2 pounds | 907 g |

## VOLUME EQUIVALENTS(LIQUID)

| US STANDARD | US STANDARD (OUNCES) | METRIC (APPROXIMATE) |
|---|---|---|
| 2 tablespoons | 1 fl.oz. | 30 mL |
| 1/4 cup | 2 fl.oz. | 60 mL |
| 1/2 cup | 4 fl.oz. | 120 mL |
| 1 cup | 8 fl.oz. | 240 mL |
| 1 1/2 cup | 12 fl.oz. | 355 mL |
| 2 cups or 1 pint | 16 fl.oz. | 475 mL |
| 4 cups or 1 quart | 32 fl.oz. | 1 L |
| 1 gallon | 128 fl.oz. | 4 L |

## TEMPERATURES EQUIVALENTS

| FAHRENHEIT(F) | CELSIUS(C) (APPROXIMATE) |
|---|---|
| 225 °F | 107 °C |
| 250 °F | 120 °C |
| 275 °F | 135 °C |
| 300 °F | 150 °C |
| 325 °F | 160 °C |
| 350 °F | 180 °C |
| 375 °F | 190 °C |
| 400 °F | 205 °C |
| 425 °F | 220 °C |
| 450 °F | 235 °C |
| 475 °F | 245 °C |
| 500 °F | 260 °C |

# Appendix 2: Recipes Index

Made in United States
Orlando, FL
16 December 2024

55688684R00043